All About
Repairing Pottery
and Porcelain

All About Repairing Pottery and Porcelain

DAVID EVERETT

HAWTHORN BOOKS, INC.
Publishers / NEW YORK

Hawthorn extends appreciation to Thelma R. Newman, author of *Crafting with Plastics*, for preparation of this edition.

ALL ABOUT REPAIRING PORCELAIN
AND POTTERY

Library of Congress Catalog Card Number: 76–5717
ISBN: 0-8015-6286-4
1   2   3   4   5   6   7   8   9   10

ALL ABOUT REPAIRING PORCELAIN AND POTTERY was originally published in the hardbound edition by Robert Hale & Company, London, as MANUAL OF PORCELAIN AND POTTERY RESTORATION. The U.S. edition is published by arrangement with Robert Hale & Company.

Contents

Illustrations

Photographs

Line figures

Preface

The ultimate way to repair pottery and porcelain is to use the original materials, clay or kaolin. In some cases, to achieve the correct texture, it is even necessary to use clay from the original location, and to fire at the same temperature in a kiln as near as possible to the one used by the original potter.

In many cases, records of firings and temperatures have been lost, or did not exist anyway. Potteries have closed down and other things have occurred to make the ultimate repair sometimes impossible, and at all times very expensive. For this reason there are very few people who undertake this type of repair, and those that do are very highly skilled, using equipment running into hundreds of dollars, and restoring only those pieces of a value that warrants the cost.

Fortunately, modern technology has come to our rescue, bringing with it materials that are cheap, easy to use and readily available, so this fascinating and rewarding pastime is now within the reach of anyone who cares to have a try, whether they have artistic skills or not.

A famous memory man once said that there is no such thing as a bad memory, only an untrained one. The same thing applies to almost anything you undertake. Taken stage by stage, the repairs covered in this book come well within the scope of the average person, especially those who have often felt the urge to do something creative, but never thought themselves capable.

The restoring of pottery and porcelain is quickly gathering impetus as both a business and a hobby, and this trend will increase as it gets more and more difficult to find pieces in perfect condition. Large manufacturing companies of resins and plastics are now taking a great interest in the subject, obviously realizing the future potential.

The antique trade imports vast quantities of pottery and porcelain each year, and this is having the effect of raising values of both perfect and restored pieces. Although it can not be said that restoring a piece also restores its full value, it certainly increases it.

There is, of course, a school of thought that restoring takes away originality. Well, to a certain extent this is true, but if the original potter were alive to choose whether a piece he made was restored or thrown away, or a plate in two halves stuck together with crude rivets or invisibly repaired, I doubt if his choice would be difficult.

1
Basic Materials

The first section of this book is devoted to simple cold repairs and painting, and a list of the materials needed. By 'cold' repairs, it is in no way implied that this section is for amateurs and the next for professionals, but merely that no heat treatment is needed. Some people will probably prefer to work this way anyway, and some jobs will be on items too large to get in a domestic oven.

All the materials mentioned should be readily available from hardware shops, model and art shops. If, for any reason they are not, a list of the manufacturers will appear at the back of the book, and they will be able to send the goods direct, or the name of your nearest stockest. Even in these days of rising costs, the materials you will need to buy are not only very cheap, but providing they are stored as directed, they will last for many repairs.

The following list is what you will need in the way of materials and tools. Doubtless you will end up adding a few more to suit your own personal style, and making or modifying others for special jobs, but these will provide a good staring point.

1. Quick setting plastic.
   Numerous brands are available, such as Devcon Five-Minute Epoxy. Sold in various size tins and tubes. A small size goes a long way.
2. Slow setting plastic.
   Sylmasta White Ceramic Plastic or Sculpey ceramic putty are the most suitable.
3. Glue.
   Elmer's, Duco, etc.
4. Epoxy resin glue.
   Araldite is probably the most famous.

5. Selection of Plastic Enamel paints.
   Flo-Paque. A selection is useful.
6. Gold Paint.
   Liquid Leaf, Flo-Paque.
7. Mixing palette.
   An expendable pad is useful, available at art shops.
8. Plasticene.
10. Elastic bands. Assorted sizes.
11. Miniature files. Useful selection as follows:
   a. $8'' \times \frac{1}{4}''$ round file
   b. $5\frac{1}{2}'' \times \frac{1}{8}''$ round file
   c. $5\frac{1}{2}'' \times \frac{1}{2}''$ half round file
   d. $5\frac{1}{2}'' \times 3/16''$ half round file .
12. Half round rasp.
13. Razor modelling knife.
14. Packet of cocktail sticks.
15. Wet and Dry Carborundum paper grades 600, 320, 180.
16. Paint brushes, watercolour type.
17. Turpentine substitute.
18. Tissues.

Quick Setting Plastic

Quick-setting plastics are available under various trade names. Devcon Corporation markets a fine selection of these materials. Under any name, the plastics set in a few minutes. The exact time depends on the room temperature and the amount of hardener used.

The kit you buy will contain a tin or tube of plastic, and a tube of hardener. Directions are always included, and it is wise to follow them closely. Too much hardener, for example, will tend to make the mixture brittle. Not enough, and it will take a long time to harden. There is a certain amount of latitude, and if you are not sure, it is better to use too little rather than too much. When it does set, it will be strong and workable, and a little extra time can be useful on intricate jobs.

Never mix very much at a time, you do not get very long to

apply it, and a lot will be wasted if you do. If the repair calls for a lot, it is better to build it up in thin layers of no more than an eighth of an inch. The hardener creates heat when mixed with the paste, and the thicker the mixture, the greater the heat generated. Too much volume will result in tiny 'blow holes' caused by bubbling, and being small these are very difficult to fill. Do not assume that the paint will fill them, because it only enhances them and ruins the look of the finished job. It is quicker to enlarge the holes with the point of the razor knife and refill them individually.

After a few minutes, the mixture will begin to stiffen, so what you have not managed to use is best thrown away. You will no longer be able to press it in to the repair nicely, so it is false economy to try and use it.

When you mix the next lot, never, under any circumstances, allow even the most minute speck of hardener to pollute the tin of plastic, or it will gradually cure, and be wasted. Take great care to wipe the mixing implement completely clean with a tissue before scooping out any more from the tin.

Always keep the lid of the tin closed when not in use, and store in a cool place. Kept well it should last for months in perfect condition.

A small piece of stiff plastic or smooth wood is ideal as a surface for mixing on. If you clean off the surplus before it hardens it will last you for ages. If a lump of plastic does harden it will often remove itself under the influence of a sharp hammer blow, or if it is on stiff plastic it may sometimes come off if you flex it. The surplus tends to build up quickly when you are busy, and allows you an ever decreasing area to mix on, so make sure you use something expendable. On anything but a waxed or glass-like surface a lump of plastic has limpet-like adhesion qualities.

Wooden cocktail sticks are ideal for mixing and applying plastics, and what is more they are cheap. Doubtless some will prefer to use proper modelling tools, it really depends on personal preference and the amount you wish to spend, but if you choose the modelling tools, take care to wipe them clean before the plastic sets. If you do get a build-up on them they will quickly become unusable and need sanding smooth. Being essentially lazy, I prefer the sticks, they are at least expendable.

Slow Setting Plastic. There are many of these on the market, and most modelling shops will be able to offer you a selection. Having tried numerous types, I found Sylmasta to be the best for my purpose. Whichever material you choose, be sure to follow the manufacturers' instructions, as they do often vary from product to product.

The companies that make these products have gone into the requirements of pottery and porcelain repair, and have ended up with eminently suitable products. Their researchers have now led them to produce putties and glazes that can be baked hard in a domestic oven, and these will be fully dealt with later on in this book.

For now we are just concerned with Sylmasta white ceramic plastic. This comes in two tins. Sylmasta A with an orange lid, and Sylmasta B with a black lid for easy identification. As the tins are of equal size, an equal quantity of each is used. Tin A which is neutral coloured contains the activator, and B contains a white mixture of epoxy resins. Only when these two components are thoroughly mixed together will hardening take place. If Sylmasta is unavailable to you, ceramic plastic or putty can be used instead.

Having taken the desired amount out of each tin, replace the lids. With all plastics, it is advisable to get into the habit of doing this as soon as conveniently possible. The reason for the different colours of each component is to make the mixing process foolproof. Only when you have rolled and kneaded the mixture into one colour, with absolutely no suspicion of streakiness is the job complete, and even then it is advisable to carry on for another couple of minutes to make sure. The hardening process will not take place evenly unless this is done.

At this stage, place the mixture on a clean surface, and wash any surplus off your hands with soap and water. If you do not do this it will tend to stick to your fingers instead of the place intended which can be most frustrating.

One of the biggest advantages of this kind of slow setting plastic is that it will remain workable for anything up to two hours in normal room temperature, so it is ideal for all jobs that cannot be done in a hurry, like hands, arms, flower petals and lots of other things.

To obtain good adhesion, it is absolutely essential to clean off any dirt or grease from the piece to be repaired. This, by the way, does not just apply to Sylmasta, but is a universal rule for anything that is to be stuck to anything else. It must also be completely dry, so wash the pottery well in warm water and detergent, and leave in a warm place to dry. Some pottery is very porous on the unglazed broken sections, so give it plenty of time to be sure. No adhesive will stick to a greasy or damp surface. When the piece is clean, try to avoid touching the broken section, even the natural oil from your skin will impair the bond.

When Sylmasta has set hard, it can be filed or sanded to shape, but it does, over a twenty-four-hour period, go extremely hard, so it is advisable to get it as near to the desired shape as possible beforehand, while it is soft. Although it may sound contradictory after all I have just said about getting the piece dry, it is a most useful feature of Sylmasta that it can be wiped smooth with a damp cloth dipped in soapy water, or a damp finger if you choose. This quality often enables you to obtain the desired shape or surface at this stage, so that when dry it is ready for decorating.

As with all plastics, wash your hands well after use. Some people have sensitive skin, and lack of care can produce irritations.

Epoxy-resin glue. This type of adhesive is so strong, if used correctly, that a bond, once cured, may be regarded as permanent. It will be unaffected by dampness or changes in temperature, and if, in the future the piece is rebroken, it will be unlikely to break on the glue joint.

Araldite is the best known epoxy-resin glue, and very simple to use. Two tubes are provided, and as they are of equal size, an equal amount is squeezed out of each tube on to an expendable mixing surface. Once again, you will notice that the two components are different colours, so that it is easy to see when they are properly mixed. There is no need to be in a hurry with this type of glue. At normal room temperature, about 60°F., it will take some twelve hours to set, and will remain fully workable for up to two hours.

Like all other plastics, emphasis must be laid on the mixing. Carelessness at this stage will mean probable failure of the bond. Also, remember to clean thoroughly the pieces to be stuck of any dirt and grease, and to have them dry and preferably warm when you apply the glue.

When you get used to using Araldite, and confident that your bonding is right first time, the curing time can be speeded up, if necessary, by heat. Placing the piece near a fire or heater will help, or if it is small enough to put in a domestic oven at 300°F. (150°C.) it will set in thirty minutes. Care must be taken though, if the piece has any value, as high temperatures may result in damage. Make sure the oven cools down before opening the door, it is the sudden change of temperature that does the damage. Unless speed is essential, it is better to allow the glue to set overnight.

To give you some idea of the strength of bond achieved with Araldite, I have a large pottery casserole that my wife placed on the direct heat on the stove. As a result, the bottom fell off, losing all the gravy in the process. Having thoroughly washed and dried it, I applied Araldite, stood the sewing machine on it to compress it nicely, and left it overnight to set. That was over five years ago, and it is still in regular use, standing the heat of the oven and washing up water without any apparent effect.

Ordinary Glues. The very permanence of an epoxy-resin bond can sometimes be its only disadvantage. If the joint is allowed to move while setting, or if it was not quite perfectly fitted in the first place, it will be most difficult to take apart. Not impossible, but time consuming and tricky.

For this reason, some people will no doubt prefer to start with an ordinary glue. There are too many on the market to name individual makes, and it will always say on the packet if it is suitable for sticking ceramics.

Most of these glues will give an adequate joint for an ornament for years, provided it is protected against dampness and receives no rough handling.

Personally, I prefer permanence and strength, but these glues do have the one advantage of giving way under the influence of hot water, so if you are unsatisfied with your first attempt, you can easily take it apart and try again.

There is no other advantage to this type of glue, so when you have read the chapter on gluing and had some practice, I would recommend an epoxy-resin because then you need have no worries about changes in temperature or dampness ruining all your efforts.

Plastic Enamel Paints. These paints, which come in handy little tins about an inch in diameter, are available from model, and most hardware shops. A large range of colours is available, which makes the task of finding the right shade a lot easier than it might otherwise be.

You will find that once you have opened the tin, a skin will form on the surface of the paint. This is because the paint cures on contact with the air. Although, as usual, it is advisable to replace the lid as soon as you can, the skin will still form. Do not keep removing this skin, because another will take its place, and this is a waste. The best procedure is just to cut a small slit in the skin with the point of a razor knife, a small amount of pressure on the skin with the handle of the knife or the blunt end of the paint brush will squeeze paint up through the slit. Use just as much as you need, and then let the slit seal itself up again. In this way the paint in your can will last a lot longer in good condition.

Most plastics go on curing for a long while after they appear to be dry, and plastic enamels are no exception, they seem to be fully set after about six weeks, at which time they are very hard. While decorating, however, only about an hour is needed before a coat can be overpainted.

These paints can be made to resemble closely the varying textures of pottery and porcelain. For the pieces with a deep glaze, a polyurethane varnish is available, and to match the duller surfaces, a matt varnish. On some occasions the paint itself will provide the necessary finish. All this will be gone into more thoroughly in the chapter on painting and colouring.

Be very careful to paint in a dust free atmosphere, or it will dry like sandpaper and be ruined. If you do not have a handy warm cupboard, it may be necessary to rig up a polythene tent or place the piece in a warm, grease free oven.

Gold Paint. Unfortunately, most of the gold paints on the market have a rough matt finish, whereas a high proportion of gilded pottery and porcelain is smooth and shiny.

The best two golds I have found are Liquid Leaf, for painting on, and Treasure Gold, which is rubbed on. Both come in a few different shades for easy matching. These two golds are quite good for reproducing the texture of gilding to be found on Oriental pieces, which tends to be duller than European gilding as the decoration is often over the glaze. Both these golds have their different uses, as will be seen later.

If you are willing to spend a bit more money, very good results can be obtained using gold leaf and applying a top coat of the clear polyurethane varnish.

Paint Brushes. Ordinary small water colour brushes are suitable for most jobs, but if you want your work to look nice do not buy cheap brushes. They shed their hair like a dog at moulting time, and leave them all over the piece you are working on. Make very sure that all brushes are cleaned immediately after use, if this is not done they will go hard and will be fit only for throwing away. Sable brushes are probably the best, but your local art shop will be able to advise you on the best he has in stock.

Turpentine. Readily available from hardware shops, turpentine, turpentine substitute or white spirit is for brush cleaning and paint thinning.

When you clean your brushes, pour about half an inch of turpentine into a small jar, old egg cup, tobacco tin or similar container. Dip the brush in, and then wipe it on a tissue, and repeat until no paint comes off on the tissue. Never clean a dirty (paint-laden) brush in the main bottle of turpentine, or you will pollute it and render it unsuitable for paint thinning.

If you are doing a lot of painting, or using many different colours, it is best to have two small containers on the go, so that one can be replaced when it is too dirty, to clean efficiently. Finally, remember that turpentine is highly inflammable, so keep it away from cigarettes and naked flames.

Mixing Palette. Any piece of stiff plastic or varnished wood will do, provided you are prepared to clean it properly and frequently. I personally find this impossible, as the paint goes touch-dry too quickly, and then it will not wipe off. I have found it more practical to use a pad of expendable grease-proof paper palettes. These are available at most art shops, and have the advantage that when you run out of mixing space, you just rip that sheet off and start on the one underneath.

Plasticene. This most useful substance, obtainable from toy shops, model shops etc., has a multitude of uses, the most common being for making moulds and supporting things that you are working on. It is very cheap, and lasts well if wrapped in foil after use.

Scotch tape. Mostly used for securing broken pieces in position while the glue is setting. It has the advantages that you can see through it, and know what is going on underneath, and that it peels off easily after use.

Some people prefer to use brown sticky paper, which is applied wet and therefore shrinks on drying, drawing the damaged pieces tightly together. This is an accepted method, and no doubt perfectly suitable, but I have always felt a bit uneasy about dampness near uncured glue. Scotch tape is easier for making support bandages around awkward places like broken arms, and where it can be stretched tight across a break, its own elasticity tends to pull the pieces together. This is another of those personal preference things, so the final choice is yours.

The basic point is that the bond is more effective if a light and uniform pressure can be applied to the joint. There are various ways of accomplishing this, which will be explained in detail in the chapter on gluing. Scotch tape is just one method, others involve elastic bands, clamps of various kinds, and even old nylon stockings.

Files. Small files are both cheap and extremely useful for obtaining the shapes you want. The list below covers the types I have found most useful, but there may well be others you will prefer to use, that suit your particular style. These can be added to your range as you go.

8″ x ¼″ round file
5½″ x ⅛″ round file
5½″ x ½″ half round file
5½″ x 3/16″ half round file

A large half round rasp is also useful. This may sound a bit big and rugged for this kind of work, but you do come across the occasional large area of quick setting plastic to be ground down on really big repairs, and a rasp is very useful for taking off the high spots and leaving a level surface to work from. The initial use of a rasp can speed this kind of job up a lot, but great care must be taken to keep it off the actual pottery, or you are liable to end up with a bigger repair job than you started with.

Knives. Stanley make an excellent expendable razor knife, with the marking 10-601 on it for identification. This knife is only about six pence, and has a slim, pointed blade which is easy to get into awkward places. Your local hardware or tool shop will probably stock it. Your carving-knife sharpener, or a fine oil stone will keep the knife in service for quite a while before a replacement is needed.

Wet and Dry Carborundum Paper. This is the material that gives you the final surface before painting. Available from hardware shops, car accessory shops and some garages.

Silicone Carbide Waterproof Abrasive Paper to give it its full title for the first and last time, shall be known from now on as wet-and-dry. The only grades you will need, from the large selection produced, are 180 for taking the worst off, 320, which is fine enough to finish all but the incredibly smooth surfaces, and lastly 600 for an ultra smooth finish to simulate a porcelain surface.

Always remember that the paint will only give an extremely thin covering to the work you have done, it will not cover up bad preparation. Your preparatory work is therefore reflected in the finished result. This is why it is necessary to finish with a very fine paper. A file will leave scratch marks, so will a coarse paper, so they must all be used in sequence.

Wet-and-dry paper, as the name implies, can be used wet or dry, and here the choice is yours. Both methods are a bit messy. If you use it dry, the paper will clog up quickly so you will use more, and you will end up with a fine dust everywhere.

If used wet, which you do by constantly dipping the paper into a bowl of water, it will last longer, and probably give you a slightly better finish, but you will get a white sludge all over the piece you are working on, your hands, trousers, shoes and carpet if you do not put paper down. This sludge is a mixture of dust and water. If it gets on to material, the water takes it right in deep making it extremely difficult to remove, so it is wise to take precautions.

When you have finished, the sludge must be washed off the piece you are working on before painting. Mostly, when you have washed it all off under clean running water, you dry the piece off and find plenty of sludge still remaining. To obtain a good finish it all has to come off, so 'repeat until clean' is the only advice I can give.

Wet-and-dry comes in 11-by-9-inch sheets. Now obviously this size folded in half is far too large to work with on what is probably a tricky little job, and you must not fold it twice, or the abrasive surfaces will come into contact and quickly wear out.

The best thing to do is to fold the sheet in half, making sure the fold is sharp, and tear it in two pieces. If you continue this process for a short while, you will end up with a piece about $2\frac{1}{4}$ in square. You will find this a handy size for most jobs when folded in half.

If you have not used an epoxy resin glue, remember to do the rubbing down process dry, or your work may well fall apart in your hand.

Very occasionally you will come across a piece with a very weak or soft glaze. For this reason it always pays to keep your rubbing down to the plastic as near as possible. Where you come across this type of glaze, it is sometimes better to rub down the border between the plastic and pottery with fine steel wool, which will not scratch the glaze. The same applies where you have stuck two pieces of glass together and wish to remove the surplus cured glue.

Another material that scratches easily is cloisonné, but we will deal with the restoring of enamels, and details of cutting and grinding equipment in a later chapter. The materials already described will be adequate to make a start with simple pottery and porcelain restoration. If you find that you enjoy it, and want to go a stage further, that will be time enough to start spending a bit more money.

2
Gluing Cracks and Breaks

A lot of the pieces I get in to restore have already been glued together, but insufficient care has been taken, and the pieces don't fit very well.

Firstly, the old repair has to be dismantled, so praying that the repairer did not use an epoxy-resin glue, the first step is to put the piece in a sinkful of hot water. If it is too large, try and get at least the glued area into the water. If you are dealing with a monster, you may have to use the bath!

Most glues will give up the fight almost immediately, and it is normally at this stage that the piece falls into a lot more pieces than you thought, the other joins having been covered in the greasy dirt so often found on old china. If you are mending the piece for yourself, this simply means you have a bigger job on your hands, but if it is for someone else it can be embarrassing, especially if they are paying for what they thought was going to be a small repair. In this instance, while the old glue is still evident to show where all the breaks were, I think it is best to contact your customer, so he can see for himself that you did not break it, and decide whether the extra work and cost is worth it.

One of the most awkward moments, when doing this work professionally, is to present your customer with a bill for ten dollars and be told that the piece is only worth five!

Experience and nosiness will soon teach you the value of various types of pottery and porcelain, but until you know, contact is always advisable if the price of the repair is to be increased.

Back to the sink. If the water is very hot, not more than a

few minutes soaking should be necessary even for the most stubborn joints, but if they refuse to come apart, clean off any surplus glue to give the water a chance to get near the break. A sharp knife will cope with the surplus.

Sometimes, the joint on a thick piece of pottery needs a helping hand, so try flexing it gently, and if there is a gap slide your razor knife in and lever it.

Should you still be unsuccessful, try boiling water, or as hot as you can get it, and leave it to soak for an hour or so. Always make sure you do not put a cold piece in to boiling water, as the sudden change of temperature may break it, so warm it up under the hot tap first.

If after all your efforts it still will not come apart, it may well be stuck with epoxy-resin glue. If so, you have a long and tedious job ahead. Not impossible, but time consuming. The only sort of solvents that will destroy an epoxy resin once cured, are chloroform and the incredibly named methylendichloride.

Fortunately, the latter chemical forms the base of some commercial paint strippers, like Red Devil and Best Brothers, and in this form it can be conveniently purchased from paint shops or do-it-yourself centres.

The method is simply to apply the paint stripper to the joint, and leave it to work, which might be anything up to twenty-four hours. If at this time the join still remains firm, pare off the softened epoxy resin with your razor knife, and any that you can remove from the actual crack, and apply more stripper. Eventually your efforts will be rewarded.

To get back to the dismantling of ordinary glues. If you are working on a piece of any age, you will notice a line of dirt around the water line. This is the greasy film that builds up on an ornament over the years, even if it has been kept in a very clean place. Whether a piece looks clean or not, it is almost certain to have this film on it, and you will remember in the notes on glue that even a hint of grease will impair the bond.

For this reason, it is vitally important to wash the piece really carefully in hot water and detergent after you have finished taking it apart. Another reason for careful washing will be more evident later, but if you are only working on a small area of the piece, filling a chip for instance, and you decorate it to the overall colour, the decoration will show up badly if it is ever washed, because the rest of it will become a lot lighter in colour.

While you are working on pottery and porcelain, in or out of the water, handle it with gentle confidence, making sure that part of your hand is underneath. When holding something like a figurine, too tight a grip might break an arm or flower, whereas too loose a grip and you might drop it, especially if the grease or detergent make it slippery. For this reason, a light, enveloping hold is best. Whatever you do, do not handle it nervously, try to cultivate the attitude that you will be careful as you can, and if the untoward happens then it is just one of those things.

The kind of precautions you can take to avert disaster, are always to make sure that you have something soft under the landing area if you drop it, a piece of sponge rubber is useful for the floor, and if you are at the sink, make sure there is only water, and not another piece of pottery underneath. A little forethought, and you will rarely have a breakage even if you do inadvertantly let go of something.

All of which brings us back, yet again, to the sink! When you have broken all the old glue joints you have to remove all the old glue. Most glues will peel off with ease, leaving you with a nice clean surface, but some of the old types of china cement may have to be scraped off with a knife. The most important thing is that every last scrap of glue is removed. You must be really meticulous about this, because if the tiniest particle is left behind the pieces will never fit properly when you come to re-assemble them.

Some china cement is the same colour as the unglazed break

1. All the old glue has been removed and the pieces cleaned

it is stuck to, and you may well have to use a magnifying glass to find the offender. Frequently it is in a corner, where the break bends at a sharp angle. Only great care in this operation will ensure a good fit later.

A word of warning. Some modern pieces of very thick pottery are very soft, so do not scrape too hard. Try for a fit first, and only scrape where there is obviously an obstruction.

Having removed all the old glue, together with any dirt that might have worked its way into the crack, give the pieces a good wash in detergent to the same consistency as you usually use for the washing up. Do not use a scouring pad, as on some pieces with decoration over the glaze you may rub the pattern off. An ordinary nylon washing-up brush is quite suitable.

When the wash is complete, rinse everything well in warm or hot water and then leave them to dry. Before you begin gluing, all the pieces must be absolutely dry. Some types of thick pottery soak up water like a sponge, and take a lot longer to dry than porcelain. Placing the pieces in a warm oven, at about 100°F. will speed the process up, or leave them overnight in a warm place.

You will notice as you go through this book that there are a lot of occasions when you have to wait for something to set or dry. This can be very aggravating when you want to get on and finish the job. I am afraid that these stages must not be hurried though. The best way to alleviate the frustration is to have quite a few jobs 'on the go' at the same time, all in different stages of completion. In this way, there is always something to be getting on with.

On with the job in hand. When you are quite satisfied that all the pieces are completely clean and dry, try fitting them together to make sure nothing has been overlooked that might stop them from fitting perfectly. At this stage it is still easy to scrape off a stubborn bit of glue, but if you jump this stage and apply the glue and then the piece does not fit, you have a very messy job on your hands.

Each piece should fit absolutely perfectly. If it does, when dry, and you are working in clean surroundings, then it will when you come to apply the glue. You must find out now to be sure of really good results.

In most cases, provided you have removed all the old glue, the pieces will fit together so well that you can only see a hairline crack. There is one other possible thing that you will only very occasionally come across that can stop two pieces from fitting properly, and that is distortion. The original process of firing causes shrinkage that sometimes sets up unequal stresses. It is often this stress that causes a piece to break where it does. In these cases, the pieces might have 'sprung'. The change of shape is only infinitessimal, but it is enough to ensure that you never get a perfect fit.

When this happens you are left with two choices. Either to be satisfied with as good a fit as you can get, or to use the grinding equipment that will be described under the more advanced techniques in a later chapter.

It is important to make quite sure that you do your glueing in clean surroundings. If you have dust, grit, or bits of old glue on the working surface, it is only too easy to pick them up on the sticky edge of a freshly glued piece and stop it from fitting perfectly.

There are a lot of people who tell themselves that they cannot do this sort of job because it is too difficult. Take it from me, the secret is care rather than skill. Anyone who is prepared to take a little time, and do the job stage by stage methodically and carefully can produce good results. There is nothing supernatural about a so-called expert, they are only people who have decided to do something and worked at it until they achieved success. They all made mistakes along the way.

If the piece to be glued is in a lot of pieces, it is best to do only two or three pieces at a time, taking great care to make sure that you do not create what is known as an undercut. This happens when due to the angles of the break, the next piece will not fit. Repairing a multiple break is rather like doing a jigsaw, except that a jigsaw has square edges so that the right piece can always be inserted from the top. In broken pottery this is not always so. It may well be that the angle of the broken edge means it can only be fitted from the inside once the pieces around it are in position. Then again, it may not fit at all. In this case it should have been fitted earlier, and unless you have grinding equipment, the only way out of the situation is to dismantle and start again. On a very complicated piece like this, it is often better to build the piece up 'dry', and use a felt-tip pen, or something that will wash off easily, to number the sequence of building. This can save a lot of time and spleen. Where necessary, support each piece with a short length of Scotch tape to hold it in position while you are experimenting with which piece to fit next.

If you intend to use Araldite, or another epoxy-resin glue, start off on simple repairs if you can. Before it cures completely, it can be soaked off with acetone. Nail varnish remover is based on the same substance, and will also do the job, but it is an expensive way to buy it.

It is hard to advise you which type of glue to use, because to some extent it depends what kind of job you are doing, whether it is for yourself or someone else and so on. I dislike the thought that I may stick something together which subsequently gets damp and starts collapsing. Probably I exaggerate the danger of this happening, but nevertheless I favour permanence, and the knowledge that a repair is as strong as it possibly can be.

A wooden cocktail stick makes a useful mixer for most jobs, but if you are going to spread the glue over a large area, a popsicle stick may be more suitable. Keep your fingers off the edges to be glued while handling them.

Araldite can be used cold or hot. Unheated it will set in about twelve hours at a room temperature of 60°F. If for some reason you are in a hurry, curing can be speeded up considerably by heat treatment. For instance the makers claim a curing time of thirty minutes if heated to 300°F in an oven. Heat of any temperature above normal room warmth will speed up the curing time, so merely standing the object near a fire will help, but if you decide to use oven temperatures, take care.

A sudden change of temperature can result in damage, so put the object in a cold oven, and let the oven cool off for quarter of an hour or so before removal.

At the start of the glueing process, you will remember that the pieces to be bonded should be thoroughly dry. It is best to apply the glue while they are still warm, as this makes the resin easier to spread. Do not be too lavish with it, or too stingy. The important thing is to cover the entire area to be bonded. Imagine you are spreading butter on to a piece of bread.

It is normally only necessary to spread the glue on to one of the two surfaces to be bonded, but if it is a thick piece of pottery, of the porous type, spread it on to both.

Having covered the area, bring the two pieces together. If you are lucky, they will immediately go into place, in which case all you have to do is to exert a light pressure to make all the surplus glue ooze out, then, to make things as easy as possible, get some help to apply the Scotch tape at right angles to the break.

The glue will tend to make the joint slippery, and if you have applied too much, it will not go into position straight away. In this case, just keep pressing the pieces together, and move them against each other gently until they are in the right position. If they fitted dry, and you have been careful not to allow any grit to get into the glue, they will fit now, so do not give up half way, just keep on pressing until you have expelled the surplus. You have to be fit for this job!

Remember, accept nothing short of perfection. When you feel that the two halves have gone together properly, apply

2. The pieces held tightly in place with tape

the tape. If no help is available, have two or three pieces about four inches long ready for use. Naturally if you cut pieces and just leave them they will curl up and be useless, so stick three and a half inches to a shiny surface, a piece of glass, or stiff plastic will do, and leave half an inch over the edge so you can peel it off easily with one hand. Stick two inches of the tape to one side of the joint, and pull it tightly as you stick it to the other half, the idea being to let the natural elasticity of the tape help to pull the two halves together. If possible, always apply the tape to both sides to even up the pull.

When you have the piece supported by the tape, try running your fingernail across the joint, to make sure there is no ridge to be felt. Always do this before applying more than one or two pieces of tape, to save having to take them all off again. Normally it is only that the joint has shifted slightly while handling, or that the tape is pulling unevenly. If you are working on your own, you may have to be a bit inventive here. There are various ways of holding the two halves together depending on the shape of the piece you are sticking.

If you are bonding the top half of a jug to the bottom half, simply stand it on a flat surface and put some weight on the top. A heavy book, an iron or some similar object will usually do the trick. Make sure after applying the weight that the joint is perfect, and leave until dry.

On something like a plate, elastic bands, a bandage, or a tourniquet made from a nylon stocking can provide a good back-up to the Scotch tape.

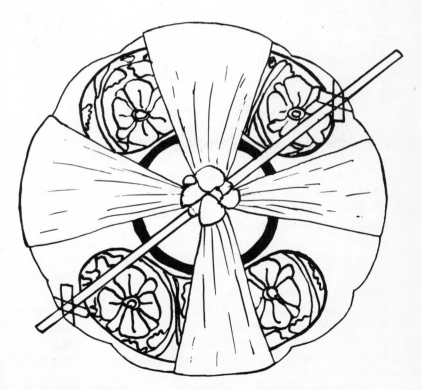

Fig. 1. A tourniquet securing the broken pieces in place

This is applied after you have a few tightly stretched lengths of tape in position to hold the two halves together. The idea, as always, is to exert a light uniform pressure. The tourniquet, as illustrated, will do the job admirably, but take care not to wind it up tight. Nylons are ideal for this job because they are a little bit elastic. When you feel you have a good firm pressure, check the joint again for ridges. If it is nice and level, tape the handle down and lock the tourniquet in place, and leave for twelve hours.

Quite often, before you get used to pressing two pieces together at the right angle, they will suddenly collapse. Resist the temptation to do anything violent, like throwing the pieces at anyone who laughs at you, and before putting the edges together for another try, make sure, if you dropped them, that they have not picked up any dirt that might prevent a perfect fit.

Never be in a hurry with this job. You have a long time to make any necessary adjustments before the glue starts to cure, so make sure it is absolutely right before and after you secure it, and check it about an hour later as well if possible, things under tension, if the tension is uneven, tend to move.

It is very difficult to explain the amount of pressure that is necessary, except to tell you to take it easy. When all the surplus has been forced out, that is probably tight enough. On some jobs I have used a carpenter's vise, but let experience teach you how tightly to screw it up — preferably on something expendable! On some jobs a wedge of plasticene pressed around each end of a joint helps to keep it level and in place while you are fixing the tape.

Some restorers use a sand box to support glued pieces while they are setting. This has the advantage of giving very even support, as the sand forms the exact shape of the piece resting on it, but great care is needed to ensure that no grit is allowed into the join, so I use various props in the form of books, lumps of Plasticene, scraps of wood and anything handy.

If you decide to invest in the 'Make-or-Break Kit', which is dealt with fully in the section on oven-baked repairs, an expoxy-resin glue is included. Although at the time of writing I have had no chance to test it, the manufacturers assure me that apart from having the same qualities as any other epoxy-glue, it can also be used as a contact adhesive.

To use it in this way, a thin smear of glue is applied to each surface, and then left for an hour. After this time has elapsed, bring the two glued edges together and they will adhere strongly enough to be self supporting.

Obviously a certain amount of care has to be taken to bring the pieces together accurately, although I am told that it is possible to adjust the fit to perfection after the pieces make contact.

There are plenty of occasions where a glue with these qualities will be invaluable, especially where support and pressure are difficult to apply.

3. Applying the glue to the broken piece

4. Fitting the pieces

5. Filling in the chips and cracks with Sylmasta

6. The finished job: the joins can just be seen on the left-hand side

On tricky jobs like figurines, it is obviously not always possible to apply pressure in all cases. Scotch tape bandages or slings will sometimes work, but if not it is often better to use quick setting plastic in the place of the glue. This sets in about ten minutes, so you can hold it in position until it is hard. This works better on pottery, which is more porous; with porcelain it is better to stay with the glue, supported in any way you can find.

When you are gluing a multiple break, and building it up two pieces at a time, take care only to apply glue to the area you are going to mate up, or the next piece will not fit. Where a bit of surplus does ooze out, let it harden and then scrape it off with a razor knife.

The surplus glue that oozes out along the joint when pressure is applied is best left until it hardens, at which time it can easily be removed with the razor knife, or rubbed flat with wet-and-dry paper as you prefer.

There is just one more case to describe in this section, and that is the incomplete crack. This is when a plate, for instance, is cracked part of the way across, but not detached. There are two alternatives. If the crack is short enough for the plate to retain its strength, the best thing is to leave it alone. On a white or light-coloured plate, if the crack annoys you because the ingrained dirt marks it show up badly, try soaking it in a solution of bleach. This often renders it almost invisible.

7. Scraping off old china cement

8. Fitting in the last of the four pieces

Where the crack is longer, and the plate flexes, it is only a matter of time before it breaks completely, so you will only be anticipating the inevitable by breaking it right across. By doing this, it is then possible to glue it together in the way described, and make it strong again. Unfortunately it is usually impossible to get glue to run into the crack unless it can be flexed quite a lot, but as this will probably break it anyway, it is best to break it first and stick it properly.

That is all, for simple glue repairs. If you have done a good job, when all the surplus is removed the join should not be noticeable from three or four feet away, and on coloured pieces not at all, unless scrutinized.

Finally, it might sound like a silly precaution, but if you have sensitive skin, use a barrier cream. Rubber gloves would be ideal, but I find that so much of this job relies on the sense of touch, that they are unsuitable. It is impossible not to get glue on your skin, so wash it off with warm soapy water when you have finished.

Another, and probably even sillier sounding precaution is to make sure the piece you are working on is pottery or porcelain! I was given a repair to do once that fooled me completely. It was a small figurine about six inches in height, and looked like poor quality white parian. This is a type of unglazed porcelain that was made by such potteries as Spode and Wedgwood. As I say, this piece of supposed parian did not look quite right, but after all, my job was only to repair it, not criticise it, so as it had already been glued up very badly, I put it in hot water, and there, right before my horrified eyes, it almost dissolved! It was made of salt, as are one or two antique figures, so beware. After an embarrassing explanation to the customer, I decided to check carefully in future, and this can easily be done by licking. It sounds unhygenic, and probably is, but it is the one sure way of finding out, and taking back a little white stump that was once a complete figure, albeit a rather poor quality one, does not endear you to the owner.

While on the subject of quality, the owner invariably thinks he or she is in possession of a real gem that they cunningly bought at a bargain price. If you decide to take up restoring professionally, you will soon get to know which pieces are valuable and which are not. From experience, disillusioning a proud owner is the quickest way to lose a customer. Much better to just charge a fair price for the repair and let them dream.

3
Filling up Chips

A chip in the rim of an ornament may be very small, but it can still completely ruin the look of it. Fortunately, they are very easy to deal with, and unless they cover a plain white area, it is usually possible to effect an invisible repair.

First things first, thoroughly wash the whole piece. In case you feel this is unnecessary, when it might just be a small chip in the top of a vase for instance, it is no use just washing the immediate area around the chip. There are two reasons for this, firstly, the vase is almost certain to have accumulated layers of grime on it, and handling it is likely to mean that some of that grime finds its way on to the repair area, where it will spoil the bond between the plastic and the pottery.

Secondly, washing a piece, as we discovered in the last chapter, lightens the colour, or rather brings it back to the original colour. This means that if you repair the chip, and then match it to the colour of the unwashed pottery, it will show up embarrassingly if the whole piece is ever washed.

This latter trap is easier to fall into than you would think, because in a lot of cases a piece looks quite clean, but if washing it only lightens it by a shade, it will still show up the repair, so always make it a rule to wash everything carefully before working on it. The finished results will more than justify the time spent.

Quick setting plastic is usually the most suitable material for filling small chips, so we will deal with that first. Assuming all surfaces are clean and dry, mix up a small quantity of quick setting plastic. Mix it well, until there are no streaks left. Now take a small amount on the end of a cocktail stick or whatever type of applicator you have decided on, and press it well into the chip. If the bond is to be good, no air gaps must remain between the pottery and the plastic, so spread it back and forth for a few seconds to make sure of a good contact. As a lot of chips are very small, it may well be possible to fill it in one mixing, but never try for a layer more than one eighth of an inch thick, or too much heat will be generated and you will end up with a lot of unsightly air holes.

If the repair is quite deep, as it could be on some thick pottery vases, you may have to apply two or more layers, which will mean waiting for the previous one to harden for about twenty minutes before mixing up more plastic and doing the next layer.

Try to get used to estimating the amount of plastic you will need. This will take a little practice, but initially you will probably tend to over-estimate and therefore have quite a lot of wastage. Remember you only have two or three minutes while the plastic remains workable, less if you are in a hot room, so do not mix up more than you can use, tend to err on the side of economy, it is always easy to mix a little more.

Once your applicator has come into contact with the hardener, which it will when you mix your first quantity, be very careful to wipe it clean with a tissue before using it to dig more plastic out of the tin. The tiniest amount of hardener to enter the tin will eventually make it go off and so it will be wasted.

However many layers you need, give the previous one time to harden properly, and score it a few times with the point of your razor knife to ensure a good 'key' with the next layer.

Always overfill the chip, as this kind of plastic always shrinks slightly, so only try for the rough shape at this stage. On very small chips, no more than $\frac{1}{8}$ inch deep, and with a surface area less than $\frac{1}{2}$ inch in any direction, the next stage can be started about half an hour after applying the plastic, but on larger areas it is better to leave it overnight by which time all the shrinkage will have happened.

In most cases, the manufacturers of quick-setting plastics claim that their product does not shrink. True, the shrinkage is very slight, and for a lot of applications it would be negligible. Unfortunately however, a lot of my customers never go anywhere without a powerful magnifying glass, and there is no doubt that if you fill a chip of any depth, and rub it down and paint it straight away, it might look perfect initially, but the next morning it will have sunk just enough to leave a clearly discernable ledge all around the repair.

Always, then, overfill the chip, leave for twenty-four hours or more, and then start the rubbing down process.

If you have made the mistake of applying the plastic too thickly, and ended up with a lot of blow holes, the best remedy is to open up each hole with the point of your knife and fill it up with more plastic. You will find it quite impossible to fill up the holes without doing this, as they are too small to force the plastic into. I do not know why, but the paint will not fill them up either, however many coats you apply, rather it tends to enhance them.

We will presume you have now overfilled the chip, and sufficient time has elapsed to enable you to start on the rubbing down process. As it will probably be a small area, 320 wet-and-dry paper will be most suitable to start with. Dip the paper into a bowl of water, and using a circular motion, rub the plastic towards the desired shape, stopping every few seconds to dip the paper into the bowl to remove the sludge from it. There is no need to press very hard, and if you are working on very thin porcelain, support it by placing your other hand under the spot you are working on.

The sludge that builds up on the paper, also accumulates on the repair area, not to mention your trousers, the carpet and the edge of the chair if you do not cover them, so if it is a small piece, dip it into the bowl at regular intervals to see how you are progressing. If it is too large to do this, wipe it with a damp tissue. Wet-and-dry paper takes only a very short time to rub down a small area of plastic, and without regular inspection you may rub off too much.

Each time you clean the area, run your finger tips over it. Get used to feeling as well as seeing. In many cases your sense of touch will find a ledge or depression that eyes would not notice.

If you ever watch an antique dealer inspecting goods he is about to buy, or value, you will notice that he always feels for possible damage at the same time as he looks. Try to cultivate this habit as soon as possible. Apart from finding flaws and imperfections, various types of pottery and porcelain have their own individual textures, and as a lot of pieces are unmarked, this can help enormously toward identification.

At first it is very likely that you will rub away too much plastic. This can be either because you were rubbing too hard, and not inspecting often enough, or because you rubbed the area flat where it should have been slightly curved (*see* fig. 2). Very few surfaces in pottery are flat, especially on the lip of an object where you are likely to find chips, so try to rub it to the right shape as you go along.

Fig. 2. The effect of too much rubbing down

The beauty of working with plastics is that it is always very easy to put right any mistakes, so if you need to add a little more, just make sure the surface is quite dry, score it with the point of your knife, and start again.

When the area of plastic is almost into shape, switch to the 600 paper for finishing off. You will find it slows down the pace of work, but it does enable you to get a really good surface, and as I mentioned earlier, paint will not disguise poor preparation. If the underneath work is good it will reflect in the finished job, and vice versa.

Remember always to use only a small piece of wet-and-dry paper folded once, and avoid scratching the surrounding area of pottery. It might feel hard, but often scratches quite badly.

All that now remains to be done is to match the colour with plastic enamel paint, and notes on the use of these paints will be found in a later chapter.

For larger or more complicated chips, for instance, those with an impressed pattern, refer to the chapter on oven baked repairs.

4

Simple Moulding

In this chapter, we shall just deal with the simple moulding jobs that can be done with the help of plasticene, like simple handles, and pieces missing from the edge of plates and vases. More complicated moulding techniques for reproducing complex things like heads, hands and ornate handles will be discussed in a later chapter.

Simple plasticene moulding is used when part of an object is missing, and the required shape is available from another part.

Let us suppose that you are going to repair a vase that has a big section missing from the top (*see* fig. 3). As long as at least half the top still remains, you can take a mould of it to give you the shape of the other half.

Using this method, the plasticene is going to give you a surface of the right curvature on which you can build up the plastic. If you are careful, you end up with one side perfect, which can be either the inside or the outside.

The first point to consider therefore is which side will be the easiest to rub down. In a narrow necked vase, for instance, it might be difficult to get at the inside. In the type of vase where

Fig. 3. (*Left*) using Plasticene to mould the correct shape and (*right*) when it is set, placing it over the damaged area

the lip is like a trumpet on the other hand, it will almost certainly be easiest to get at from the inside. Where the glaze is soft and liable to scratching, it may well be advisable to take a mould of the outside and put up with any inconvencience there may be rubbing down from the inside. Work out a plan before you start and then you can always do things the easiest way if there is one.

Make sure the piece of plasticene you use is of ample size to cover the required area with an overlap of an inch or so, and that it is free from lumps of grit or anything that might impair the mould. It should be soft and workable, and if it is not, work it in your hands for a few minutes or leave it near some heat. A word of warning though, from one who has suffered. If you decide to put it under the grill or in the oven to soften, do not over do it, and approach it with caution. If it is too hot, and you grab it, you cannot drop it! It will stick to your skin

9. Making a new lip from Sylmasta

10. Trimming off the surplus with a razor knife

and carry on singeing you until you scrape it off. Very painful!

So, get the plasticene warm rather than hot, and roll it out so that it will cover the missing section with about an inch to spare all round, whilst the thickness can be somewhere between $\frac{3}{8}$ inch and $\frac{1}{2}$ inch.

The next stage demands extreme care, because the moulding surface needs waxing or oiling so that it will 'release' easily. Naturally, if the oil is allowed to get on to the broken surface of the pottery the plastic will not stick to it, so only a smear is needed, and when you have applied it make sure you clean it off your hands. As to what to use, furniture polish, or Vaseline will do the trick.

We will assume that you have decided to use the inside surface for moulding, and apply the plastic from the outside. Take the plasticene pad, and press it, oily side first, into the good part of the vase. Press it on firmly, making sure that when removed and placed over the missing area, it will cover all of it. If you are working on thin porcelain, use the usual care when pressing on part of it, and support it from behind.

The plasticene now needs to be cooled down so that it will go stiff. If possible, place the whole object in the fridge for half an hour or so. Where the piece is too large, put it in a cool place and leave it until the plasticene has gone hard. Overnight should do. When you come to remove it, the oil should make it release easily, but occasionally, faults or pockmarks in the pottery make it cling a little, so try and ease it off without altering the shape. When it is off, if you think you have bent it or stretched it a little, smear some more polish or oil on it and press it back for a second just to regain the shape, and take it off immediately.

When you are quite satisfied that you have the correct shape, place the plasticene over the missing section, and fasten it into position with Scotch tape.

It may sound like a lot of unnecessary work getting the

plasticene hard, but if you place it over the missing section while it is still soft, the outline of the jagged edge will bite into it, so that when you take if off, instead of being a nice flush fit, the plastic will be slightly lower than the surrounding pottery and need building up level.

Having secured the plasticene in position, mix up some quick setting plastic. Remember that surface you are going to spread it over is oily, and that you do not want any oil to mix with the plastic, so spread the first layer on in one movement if you can, to a depth of not more than $\frac{1}{8}$ inch and then leave it to set. The idea being not to risk turning it over and thus mixing oil with the plastic.

If you can cover the whole area with the first layer, so much the better, but if not, just hold it horizontal and let gravity help it into position while it sets, and then mix more plastic and continue to build it up in thin layers until the whole area is overfilled, finally leaving it for at least twenty-four hours to shrink.

This will be a larger area of plastic to rub down than you have done so far, so depending on size, you will need to start the job with the rasp, surform rasp, or 8-inch round file.

For most jobs the latter will do, the larger tools only being necessary where the area of plastic exceeds about two inches in width. There is a very good reason for starting off with a long file. Almost certainly, the plastic will have undulations in it, and where a small piece of wet-and-dry will follow the contour of the bumps, a long file will flatten them.

It is of paramount importance to get the whole area flat and level at this stage, because if you do not get the shape right the end results will never look good. While we are on the subject of shape, remember that you are working on a curved surface. The simplest type of curve is to be found on the cylindrical vase. Here, you only have one curve to worry about, and it is this curve where most mistakes usually occur, because it is very easy, if you are in too much of a hurry, to flatten the curve (*see* fig. 2).

Before you start to file, take off the plasticene. This should release quite easily, but sometimes, for various reasons, it is a little stubborn. If you are working on thick, strong pottery, you can afford to be a bit rough with it. If you work your way round it peeling it up at the edges, this should do the trick, but if it does not, or if the piece is rather delicate, warm it up. This will enable you to take most of it off easily, and the remains can be scraped off with a cocktail stick. Do not, whatever you do, scrape it off with a knife, as you will scratch the plastic. Any lingering traces of plasticene can now be wiped off with a tissue dampened with turpentine.

The inside surface of the plastic should now be nice and smooth, and in exactly the right shape, and this will be a good guideline for filing the outside.

Use your files in sequence. Take the high spots out with the rasp or long file. If you choose the file, use it with a diagonal motion, drawing it back and forth in the same track would only make a small trench. Do not press hard, and take care not to touch the pottery, especially with the rasp, or you will knock chips off it.

When you have taken off the high spots, stop and take a look at your work. If you think that most of the contour is right, but there are still a few low spots or depressions, it may be that these places need to be filled up. As the surface should already be fairly rough, there will be no need to score it, but make sure to blow the dust out before applying more quick setting plastic. As usual, build up slightly overfull and leave it to set. If it is only a thin layer, you can file it down after twenty minutes or so, otherwise it is yet another twenty-four hours wait!

Beware of the dust while filing, it gets everywhere, so do not do it near any wet paint. Quite often, the file gets clogged up with it and has to be cleared to remain efficient. There are numerous ways of doing this, a sharp tap against a piece of wood will often do the trick, but do not hit it against metal or it might snap, files tend to be rather brittle. A bowl of warm water and a scrubbing brush is another way, but sometimes the only thing is to painstakingly clear it with a knife point.

If you are working near wet paint, and have no alternative, the dust can be avoided by treating the file as though it were wet-and-dry, and dip it regularly into a bowl of water. Take care to wash and dry the file as soon as you finish though, or it will go rusty. In summer time, I make a habit of doing as much of the 'dirty work' as possible out in the garden.

Presuming you have re-filled any depressions, and they are now ready for filing, gently rub them down level. Whether you are using a file, or wet-and-dry, it always seems that the plastic is taking ages to be filed off until suddenly you have taken off too much. The secret is to apply only a light pressure at all times, you have to pay dearly for too much haste in the restoring business!

Filing a single or multiple curve to the correct shape is not easy, and you will probably make a few mistakes at first, I know I did. The only advice I can give you is to take it slowly, and to stop at regular intervals to check. Obviously the smaller the area to be rubbed down, the easier it will be to achieve the correct shape. The main thing is that whenever you slip up and remove too much, it can be easily replaced, so you can have as many tries as you like.

Never try to file it right down to the required level, leave it slightly high, and finish off with wet and dry paper. If you do not, the scratch marks left by the file or rasp may go down too far, and they will still be there when you have achieved the final surface.

Start off with 180 to remove the scratches, and follow with 320 and finally 600. Dip the paper regularly to let the sludge float off, and if you have folded it once, as advised, you will be able to swap sides when the first side goes blunt, as it will after a while.

When you are happy with the shape and surface, wash it well under running water. It usually happens that if you have any craters in the surface the sludge will fill them up, and so they will not notice until washed. If this has happened, and it often does, dry the piece well, fill the holes with quick-setting plastic and rub down when set.

Your surface should now be looking nice and smooth, so before you go any further, run your finger tips over it in each direction. Probably because of the dull matt surface of the plastic, imperfections like slight changes in level, and ridges where the plastic meets the pottery are often more easily felt than seen.

Any imperfections must be put right at this stage, far from covering them up, paint only highlights them. There is just no way to do this job quickly, until you get good enough to get it right first time. Just remember to score the surface before applying more plastic, and keep filling and rubbing down until you are satisfied with the result.

Some people find it easier to use a small rubbing down block to wrap the wet-and-dry around, and the ideal thing for this is a large india eraser about two inches long, the type you used to use at school. It can be easier to get a flat surface this way, where the pressure of your finger tips through the paper may make depressions. This is one of those personal things where you will soon decide what suits your style best. Nearly all the surfaces you will work on are curved, and I find that a rubbing block tends to make 'flats' in the curve.

The thing to bear in mind is that if you do not get it right at once, it does not really matter. Patience is far more important than skill. If your preparation is good, you will be delighted by the way a well matched colour can hide some repairs completely, and make others acceptable.

Painting is the easy part, the finishing touch. For a lot of people it is the most enjoyable part of the job, but it is most frustrating when it shows up all sorts of defects. At the risk of boring you, remember, perfect results depend on perfect preparation.

Another good case for plasticene moulding is where a two-handled vase has one handle missing. This is a common repair, as handles are very vulnerable to damage.

Take a nice big wedge of warmed and softened plasticene, smear the handle with wax or Vaseline for easy releasing. The Plasticene should, by the way, be roughly pre-shaped so that firstly, it is larger in area than the handle, and secondly, it is thick enough to take an indentation of half the handle leaving another $\frac{1}{2}$ inch for strength.

Supporting the handle so you do not snap that one off as well, press the plasticene in from one side, a little over half way. Now imagine a line drawn down the centre of the handle, take your razor knife, and cut down that line. Now remove the handle, taking care not to distort it. If necessary, put it in the freezer for a few minutes to stiffen it. Now cut the piece that you could not get at because it was inside the handle, down to the same level. You should now have a mould of exactly half the handle, so repeat the process from the other side for the other half.

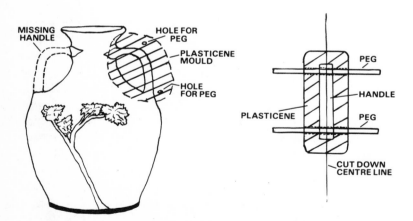

Fig. 4. Moulding a handle

Both halves of the mould should be cooled to make sure they are fairly stiff. If any traces of Plasticene remain on the vase handle, wipe them off with turpentine, dry, and re-wax, or these might stick to the inside of the mould during the next stage, and impair the surface. Having done this, place both halves of the mould, having previously waxed the surfaces that will come into contact that is, into position, and stick at least two cocktail sticks through both halves, taking care to miss the handle. Now take the sticks out and remove the mould.

You are now ready to fill the two halves of the mould with quick-setting plastic, so first wax both halves, and then mix enough plastic to fill them both. In this instance, you are going to have to mix an ample quantity and never mind the wastage, because you probably will not have time to mix up a second lot if you do not make enough.

Press the plastic firmly into each half of the mould, filling just above mould level. Now put the two halves of the mould together, and put the cocktail sticks into place to ensure correct alignment. Now put the whole thing into place on the vase, and ignoring any surplus that may squeeze out, and using elastic bands or tape, secure it in position for half an hour.

You may have difficulty in positioning the mould on the vase. This really depends on whether any part of the handle remains. If there is a couple of stumps, this will ensure alignment. If not, try making the top of the mould reach just over the lip of the vase, so it will fit straight into the right place.

After half an hour, take out the cocktail sticks, and part the mould. You will most likely be appalled at the sight that initially meets your eyes, but if you look again you should find that it is only the surplus plastic that squeezed out that is making the handle look so odd. These bits will only be wafer thin, and will be easily pared off with the razor knife.

As you had to mix up a lot of plastic, you will probably have a few little blow holes which will have to be filled and rubbed down, but after this, you should have a very respectable handle.

Do not worry if your new handle broke off while removing the mould. In a way this is a good thing, because you can stick it back on with Araldite. On some porous surfaces the quick setting plastic sticks very well, but it is as well to test it, while holding it over something soft, by picking it up with the new handle, or try and waggle it off if you like, if you do not someone else might at a later date, and they will not have the advantage of knowing it might part company with the vase!

5
Modelling

I could have entitled this chapter 'Sculpting', but if I had I could imagine a lot of people saying that the whole thing is getting far too advanced and technical.

At this point I want to stress again that nearly all these jobs come well within the capabilities of most people. Do not be put off by high flown titles, you can probably do it if you try. Attempt everything, and do not lose heart if some of the more difficult things do not work to begin with. Using these materials you can have as many tries as you need, and if you approach each stage in sequence as described you will be surprised how easy it will become.

As an example of one of the most difficult jobs you will come across, let us suppose that you have a pottery figure with one arm completely missing. A very common complaint with pottery figures.

There is one big factor to your advantage – that nearly all the information you need to make a new arm can be gleaned from the remaining arm. The size, length, thickness, colour etc. And most important, detail and quality. Some pottery figures are quite crude in their modelling. If so, yours must be just as crude, because the idea is to make a replica.

One of the secrets of this business is simple observation. This is vitally important. Most of the work is concerned with copying, whether it is colour, shape, size or quality.

To give you an example of what I mean, I got a Staffordshire figure in to repair some time ago, to replace a hand. Now Staffordshire figures were originally made as cheap ornaments. They have since, like the china figures that used to be given out as prizes at fairgrounds, become collectors pieces, and I have no wish to offend collectors when I say that they are quite crudely made. The hands, for instance, are just flat pieces of clay, with slight depressions to indicate fingers, with no pretence at detail.

On this particular job, someone had built a very nice hand with finely chiseled knuckles and finger nails and so on. The quality of the modelling was absolutely first rate, quite worthy of a Chelsea or Bow porcelain figure, but looking awfully out of place on a piece of Staffordshire. It must have taken hours as well!

Look, therefore, very carefully at the piece you are about to reproduce, and aim to make yours no better or worse.

The first step is to get hold of some thin but rigid wire, and cut it to the exact length of the remaining arm, from the shoulder to the centre of the palm. I am presuming, of course, that the missing arm is broken off at the shoulder. If part of it is still there, allow for the shorter length.

Fig. 5. Positioning a new arm with a piece of wire

Before you go any further, the position of the missing arm must be established. We will presume that the piece has only just come into your possession, and so you do not know.

There are numerous ways of resolving this problem, and only by being very careful will you end up with an arm that looks completely natural. In some cases it is obvious, such as where the arm was resting on some other part of the body, and there is a spot of rough pottery where it was in contact. In this instance, by positioning the wire arm in a few different attitudes, with the elbow carefully measured off from the good arm, it is usually possible to end up with a natural position.

Natural is the key word, if a limb is out of proportion, or bent in to an unlikely position, it will never look right, even if it is painted superbly. Most people, at some time in their lives, have had a try at drawing human figures, and found it extremely difficult, even when copying from a model, to obtain a good likeness. Admittedly, some have that magical quality that enables them to draw anything and make it look right. I wish I was one of them.

For those of you like me, who cannot draw or sculpt, do not be misled into thinking that this sort of modelling is beyond your capabilities, there are many ways to make it easier.

One of the most useful items to help you, is a pair of dividers (the type used in schools will do) for transferring measurements. This tool will enable you to mark accurately the distance between the shoulder and elbow, elbow and wrist, and when the time comes, the palm and fingers. So you see, whereas the natural born artist can do these things automatically, you can do them mechanically and achieve the same results. You have, in this case, the remaining arm. And this arm contains all the measurements you need.

If your measurements are right, the matter of positioning is made far more easy. An arm that is too long, or too short, or out of proportion between upper arm and forearm, would not look right whatever position you choose, so begin by carefully marking off the elbow from the shoulder, and putting a small bend in it. Next, with a scratch, or ring of paint, mark the wrist joint.

You now have a piece of wire of exactly the right dimensions, and all that remains is to position it correctly. Make sure, by the way, that it is straight in between the joints. To look right it must only be bent where a real arm bends, and this brings us to another point. The real thing makes a pretty good model. On more than one occasion I have put myself, my long-suffering wife, or any other available human in to the position of the pottery figure. Nine times out of ten, the arm that you are trying to reproduce falls naturally in to an acceptable position, or if it does not, get your model to try a few alternatives until you find one you like. Make sure while you, or a model if you have one, are trying out different positions, that the rest of the body is kept as near as possible to that of the figure. This cuts down the possible choices considerably. When you have made a decision, simply bend the wire to the same position.

Really, this is an exercise in observation. You will have often seen yourself in a mirror, but have you noticed which is the longer, your upper or lower arm? Is your palm longer than your fingers? It helps greatly in the modelling of figures to know the proportions of your own limbs. Note for instance, the way your arm bends at the elbow and shoulder, the position of your forearm when your arms are outstretched palms uppermost, and how it changes when you turn your hands over. All this sort of knowledge will help you to make a better job of the arm you are making. Remember, that above all else, the new arm must look natural. It does not need to be very far out of position to look ungainly.

It is always possible that the figure you are working on is well known, quite a few of the large potteries made series of certain figures and sold thousands. A reference library of

11. Mixing the glue of the make-or-break kit

illustrated books on antique pottery is very useful. At one time
these sort of books used to illustrate only priceless collectors
pieces, which was not much help for the average restorer, but
nowadays it is realized that the normal enthusiast can not
afford to pay thousands of dollars, or even hundreds for that
matter for a piece to add to his collection, and there are quite a
few books giving illustrations of a wide range of all qualities
of pottery. It is always worth looking through these books to
see if you can find a picture of either the same figure you are
working on, or a similar one to copy from.

For this type of repair, the best thing to use is Sylmasta slow
setting plastic, and in this instance the setting time can be
speeded up. One kit that recently has been made available is the
Make-or-Break kit. Short of power tools, this kit will give you
all you need for oven-baked repairs. It includes, apart from
ceramic putty, pigments and glazes, glue, thinners, a razor

knife and a paint brush. However, if the kit is unavailable in your area, you can, of course, purchase the contents of the kit separately.

So far, I have avoided the oven-baked repairs, because some people will prefer to use a quick setting plastic, and some vases and figures are too large to go into a domestic oven, so quick-setting plastic and plastic-enamel paints would have to be used. I said earlier in the book that different materials suit different jobs, but where you can get a piece into the oven, the pigments and glazes in the make-or-break kit will give a far more professional finish that will be as scratch proof as the real thing.

Until these low-temperature glazes came out, one of the disadvantages of ordinary plastics has been that although they set very hard, they can still be scratched with a knife, and the alternative was to use proper potters' glazes and a potter's kiln. Apart from the more obvious disadvantage, that of cost, the very high temperatures involved could damage an old piece beyond repair. With these new low-temperature glazes, an ordinary domestic oven is all that is required, and unlike a potter's kiln, this is to be found in practically every household.

More about the pigments and glazes later, for the time being we are concerned with building an arm around the wire skeleton you have made, and for this we will use Sylmasta, and the choice will be yours whether you fire it or not. The difference is about five hours setting time.

Mix the Sylmasta as instructed, making sure the two parts are kneaded together until they are one uniform colour. At first, mix just enough to make a thin arm, and slide it over the wire. Press it well into the broken shoulder, that you will, of course, have washed and dried as usual. A couple of cocktail stick props will probably be needed to stop it from flopping.

If any of the Sylmasta has been pressed into an awkward place like under the arm pit, and will come outside the final contour of the arm, take it off with the knife at this stage.

Fig. 6. (*Left*) making a 'thin arm' and (*right*) the final arm built up around it

When it sets, it is as hard as iron, so give yourself as little filing and rubbing down to do as possible.

The cocktail sticks, which should be wooden ones if you are going to fire it, will make little holes, but the whole area of the arm is going to be covered up, so do not worry. All you need to do at this stage is to get the thin arm pressed well home at the shoulder, and fixed into the right position.

When you have done this, either leave it for six hours to set, or put it into a cold oven, set the thermostat for 250° F. Leave it at this temperature for ten minutes, and then switch off and leave it to cool for twenty minutes. Remember, that sudden changes of temperature are what damage pottery rather than heat, so do not put a cold piece into a hot oven, or open a hot oven and let cold air in. Always allow it to cool somewhat first.

The reason for making a thin arm at first, is to get it stuck on to the shoulder and in position. It is now quite a straightfoward task to mix up more Sylmasta and build up the arm to the correct shape. While you are doing this, it is quite possible, if care is not taken, to snap the new arm off at the shoulder while pressing on the new layers of plastic. This does not really matter, because it can always be stuck back on again with Araldite, or if you are using the make-or-break kit, the epoxy-resin glue provided. If you pressed the Sylmasta well up in to the broken surface in the first place, you will already have a perfect fit. It might be a good idea to check that the broken surface is free from grease, dirt, or anything else that might have caused the Sylmasta not to stick properly in the first place.

Although modern glues and plastics give extremely strong bonds, they do, of course, need a reasonable area of contact to give the strength they are capable of. It would not be enough for instance just to put a blob of glue on the end of the wire, press it against the pottery, and expect it to stay put afterwards if any pressure is applied. For this reason, when you build a thin arm around the wire, make sure it is as thick as the real arm at the point of contact, and this will give a good strong bond.

If you start to do this work professionally, you may, for the sake of speed, wish to leave out the 'thin-arm' stage. If so, you will need the tools to drill a hole into the pottery to fit the wire into. Fairly rigid wire, pressed in to a snug fitting hole with Araldite will give an amply strong skeleton to build up the arm on. There is a chapter on drilling and grinding tools later in the book.

Like most other hobbies, you can spend as much money on it as you like. Fortunately, it is possible to do the majority of jobs on a very small outlay, and I am going to assume that you will approach it this way. Short cuts and improvements that can be done with the use of power tools will be dealt with later, for the benefit of those who wish to use them.

We are at the stage then, where you have a thin arm of Sylmasta-clad wire, that is only thickened up near the joint with the pottery. For the time being, it is best to concentrate on the arm, and leave the hand until later. You will remember that the wire was measured to the centre of the palm, so leave this sticking out as a peg on which to fit the hand when you make it.

If the arm is clothed, and ends in a cuff, this will be a suitable point to build down to. If it is bare, finish it at the wrist, and in both cases leave the rest as your peg for the hand.

Sylmasta remains workable at room temperature for over an hour, so do not hurry while you are modelling. Take frequent checks with the dividers to ensure that the measurements from shoulder to elbow and elbow to wrist do not alter as you build the thickness up, and check the thickness from the good arm in the same way.

Apart from creative ability, I think it is probably fair to say that the main difference between a good artist and a mediocre artist is observance. A good artist sees things in proportion. He probably even sees things three dimensionally where most of us see only flat objects. The main thing is, that he *sees* things, he notices the details that make the finished result look right.

In restoration, your job is usually considerably easier than that of the artist, because you have something to copy from. In the case of the arm under construction, we will imagine first of all that it is clothed in a sleeve.

If you study the good arm, you will notice that the sleeve has deep creases on the inside of the elbow bend where the material is slack, whereas on the outside of the bend the sleeve is stretched, so there are no creases. The sharper the angle at which the elbow is bent, the deeper the concertina of creases on the inside, and the more protruberant the elbow bone on the outside.

Your new arm may well be bent at a different angle to the good arm, so once again, use yourself as a model. Wearing a shirt or jacket or whatever the figure is wearing, bend your arm to the same angle and see where the creases appear. Not just around the elbow, take a good look at the armpit and all the other parts of the arm as well.

We will presume that after taking careful measurement, you have arrived at the point where you have a nice round arm of the correct length and thickness. If you now indent the creases in the right places you will be amazed at the difference. The arm suddenly begins to look lifelike.

One very important factor for success, do not be frightened to have a go. If you are putting a crease in, make it deep enough to notice, always in keeping, of course, with the good arm. If you do not like it, it can always be altered, bent to a different angle, narrowed or broadened while the plastic remains workable. The great asset of Sylmasta is that it takes on a really smooth surface if you work it with damp tools or fingers, so with care at this stage you can complete the arm ready for firing in the oven.

For a few dollars, an art or modelling shop will sell you a modelling tool rather like a rat's tail. The tapering diameter of this tool will enable you to impress sharp, deep or shallow creases quite easily. Whatever you decide to use, however, keep dipping it in water to stop it sticking to the Sylmasta.

More than likely, if you are anything like me, your first, and maybe second and third efforts will be far from perfect, but they will serve to give you practice, and experience at handling the material. If you are not happy with the result, try and see why. Sit in front of a mirror again if necessary, and compare the position of the creases and the depth. Check your measurements again from the good arm. Whatever you do, do not give up after the first few efforts. You may well find that you have a natural talent and quickly you become very good, but you may equally find that you become very good after a lot of practice.

To illustrate this very point, I visited a long-standing customer a short while ago, and on the mantelpiece I noticed a figure that was one of the first 'arm-and-hand' jobs I ever attempted. Making the rash mistake of taking a closer look, I was appalled to find that the arms were in unnatural positions, and the hands were like two bunches of bananas! Just looking at it covered me with embarassment, and the more I tried to ignore it, the more my unwilling eyes were drawn back to the ghastly thing. In the end I could stand it no longer, I took it home with me, performed two quick amputations, and did the job again.

When I had completed it, two very significant points emerged. Firstly, I had improved a lot with practice, and secondly I had noticed how awful it had looked, which might, on the face of it seem a stupid point to bring out. The thing is, when I did the job originally, I had obviously thought it looked alright, which means that in those days I must have been very much lacking in observation.

If the arm you are making is bare, the features calling for special observation are the muscles, and the way they change shape as the arm is moved into different positions. As usual, the amount of shape and detail you can put in depends very much on the good arm, and how elaborate or crudely it is made.

The outside of the arm, the section that will probably show most, gets its shape from the bicep and forearm muscles. It is sometimes a good plan to exaggerate these muscles at first by building them too large, and then smooth them down to the desired shape and size gradually with a wet finger. This tends to teach you exactly where the muscles are, and in turn, make you more observant and critical. It is quite amazing how you can look at something without seeing it until you try to make it or draw it. Each time you realize something is wrong and then put it right, your powers of observation improve along with the standard of your work.

The beauty of Sylmasta for this kind of job is that it is the only plastic on the market that can be smoothed or shaped with damp tools while it remains workable. This means it can be handled without it sticking to your skin and being pulled out of shape or covered in fingerprints. If you let your fingers or tools get dry inadvertantly and mar the surface, it can easily be smoothed down again by wiping with a damp object i.e., finger, modelling tool or sponge.

When you are happy with the arm, put the figure in a cool oven, heat up to 250°F., keep it at this temperature for ten minutes and then let it cool for twenty minutes or so.

On most modern electric ovens, a light comes on when you switch on, and goes off when the required temperature is reached, and it is from then that your ten minutes starts. Obviously this timing is only a guide, and there will be some leeway, but it should be followed as nearly as you can. If you do not have a light, or any other means of knowing when the 250° is reached, it should suffice to put the figure in a cold oven and switch on, leaving it for twenty-five minutes and then switching off and starting the twenty-minute cooling period. Remember never to put a cold object in a hot oven, or open a hot oven and let cold air rush in.

Having baked and hardened the arm, it is not too late to do any necessary alterations, it can still be filed or rubbed down with sandpaper or wet-and-dry. It does, however, set very hard, so if with practice you can finish it before baking, so much the better. If you need to add some more Sylmasta, it can be baked all over again without harm to the previously baked arm. There is no disadvantage to over-baking, except that it can yellow the plastic slightly, but as you will be colouring and glazing it later this is irrelevant.

The next job is probably the most difficult you will ever come up against in restoring things, and that is the hands. As I mentioned earlier, hands on pottery and porcelain figures vary from shapeless splodges to finely detailed ones with knuckles, fingernails and everything.

If you have the misfortune to start off on the small and

highly detailed type, you have a painstaking job on. My first attempt looked like something out of *Dracula*. My next effort was not much better and my third made me wonder if I should not take up a new hobby altogether.

At first I could not make this out, until I took a good long look at my own hand and made a few discoveries. Firstly I noticed that it was not flat after all, and that the thumb has its root down by the wrist, and not next to the index finger. Also, the thumb in a relaxed hand lies below the index finger, not beside it. The fingers always have a curl in them unless they are forced to be straight.

In a figure, the hands are invariably relaxed unless they are holding things, and even the fingers are seldom straight. After taking stock of all these things I should have noticed in the first place, my hands started improving a lot. I also found myself looking a lot more closely at all sorts of things, and deriving a lot more pleasure and appreciation from all objects of beauty.

I have made a few diagrams showing the back and palm of an outstretched hand, to give an idea of the comparative dimensions. Of course, not all hands are the same, and if you have a good hand on the figure to take measurements from it is

Figs. 7, 8. The dimensions of the hand

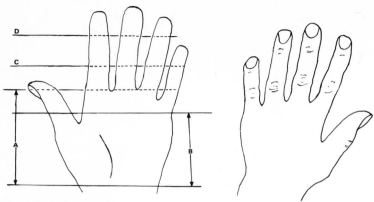

Fig. 9. The dimensions of the hand

best to do so, but if not, this will serve as a guide.

A and B shows the difference between the length of one side of the palm and the other. Also, note that the first joint of the little finger almost lines up with A, as do the knuckles of the other three fingers. C lines up with the second joint of the little and the first joint of the others and D lines up with the end of the little finger and the second joint of the others.

It is most important to recognise that on nearly all hands, all the fingers are different lengths. Nothing looks worse than a modelled hand where they are all the same length, this is when they take on the look of a bunch of bananas. Also, the fingers do not taper all that much on most hands, and the thumb in some cases actually widens towards the nail.

Figure 10 shows a suitable method of cutting out the pieces of plastic to make up a hand. Doubtless there will be those who will prefer to make up a hand from one piece, and if you find this is a better method by all means use it. Personally, I have tried both, and ended up in favour of cutting out all the pieces separately as in the diagram. In this way, each finger can be rolled out round and slightly tapered, so that when attached to the palm it is already the right shape.

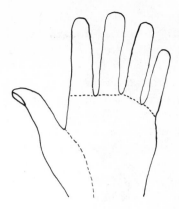

Fig. 10. Cutting out the different portions of the hand

I have presumed all the way through that you have a good hand on the figure to take your measurements from. If this is not so, a good guide to determine the length of the hands is to make them from wrist to fingertip two-thirds as long as the forearm from wrist to elbow, and to make the palm as long and as wide as the longest finger.

Naturally it is very important to get things in their correct proportion to look right. Being fiddly things to make, one is tempted to make the hands larger than they should be to make the job easier. On one of my earliest efforts I made the fingers almost twice as long as the palm, and had to take careful measurements with the dividers to find our why they looked so weird.

From that time on, I made constant use of the dividers for measuring the length, breadth and depth of everything I had to model, so at least the proportions were right. This brings me to point out to those who feel that this part of restoring is beyond them, that if careful measurement can ensure that everything looks right as far as size is concerned, then only one more aspect is needed to achieve a very high standard, and that is the quality of modelling.

If proportions are right, at least half the battle has been won, and as Sylmasta can be rubbed down even when hard, and is easy to shape when soft, care and practice can give the same results as natural skill.

When the Sylmasta is first mixed, the process of hardening begins, and after about half an hour the texture is more suitable for modelling complex items. At this stage, it is still soft enough to retain all the advantages of adhesion and can still be smoothed with a damp tool, while at the same time it is not so floppy and more able to support itself.

The palm can be made flat initially, but deeper at the wrist end. Lay it on a damp piece of paper to avoid sticking. Now the little finger may be rolled out and pressed gently into place with a wet cocktail stick, smoothing around the join at the same time. The palm, by the way, is usually laid on its back for this operation so you complete the inside surface of the hand first. Repeat the process for all the other fingers and finally the thumb, making sure that you just press each one in gently around the roots, and do not alter its length.

As the fingers on the figure are bound to curl in the manner of a naturally relaxed hand, it is doubtful that the inside will show very much on the finished job. The outside is far more important to get perfect, and for this reason combined with the inaccessibility of the inside of the hand once in position it is important to get the joints smoothed on to the palm first.

When this has been done, wet another piece of paper, newspaper is ideal, lay it over the hand and then turn both pieces over. If the first piece of paper was nice and wet, it should now peel off easily, leaving you with the hand on the second piece palm downwards. Take care in peeling the paper off though, if it has dried out it will damage the hand, so in this case wet it down again before carefully rolling it off.

As the Sylmasta will still be soft at this stage, the hand complete with thumb can be finished while it is laying flat on the paper. With a wet cocktail stick, make sure that all the joints are closed up and smoothed over, adding more Sylmasta to build up the knuckles if necessary, depending on the amount of detail required. As a general guide, the more the fingers are curled the more the knuckles stick out. Note this from your own hand. Fortunately very few porcelain figures include such details as the finger nails, or the loose skin on the back of the joints on a straightened finger, so you will rarely have to go this far.

You now have a complete but flat hand, which has to be fitted on to the wire you have left sticking out of the wrist. The question is, when to put it there? This largely depends on the final position of the fingers and thumb. By this time, the Sylmasta will have stiffened up to the extent that it will probably feel self supporting. If it is no longer soft and sticky to the touch, lift it carefully off the paper, and gently push it on to the wire and up into the required position, if necessary, using a little freshly mixed Sylmasta to smooth over the join. The thumb section can now be bent over at right angles to the back of the hand, and the fingers given the desired amount of curl. You will notice from your own hand that the little finger tends to curl most when relaxed and the index finger least. The thumb, which remains almost straight, may well touch the end of the index finger.

Your attendance is required until the Sylmasta has gone fairly hard. If you go too far away, you may well find that the fingers you positioned so nicely have, half an hour later, wilted like dying flowers, and if rigor mortis has set in it may be too late to re-position them. Stay on hand, therefore, to correct any flopping before it is too late. It is terribly frustrating to ruin the job at this stage!

Temperature decides the setting time of plastics, so when you are satisfied that you have got the hand at the right angle (the position of the forearm will govern this) and the fingers in the required attitude, the more heat you can apply, the quicker the plastic will set. Obviously the oven is the best bet, but if yours does not have a glass inspection panel, leave the door open and watch like a hawk for any sign of drooping, and correct it immediately.

Drooping or flopping is far more easily controlled when the hand is holding something. Let us suppose, for example, that it is holding the shaft of a spear. This not only governs the position of the fingers (and the arm and wrist as well) but also supports them while setting. In this instance, always remember that the shaft will come between the thumb and index finger. This sounds obvious, but it is easy enough to forget and wrap the thumb around the same side as all the other fingers which looks most odd.

If you have to make the spear, make it first, so that it is good and hard by the time you come to fit it. A good way to make a straight, thin object like this is to impress the shape into plasticene, roll out the Sylmasta, lay it in the groove, and leave it overnight.

When everything has set, there may well be some small modifications or improvements necessary. Should you need to build up more thickness, simply mix up more Sylmasta, lay it on the required place and smooth damply into shape. Where excess needs removing, use a file or wet-and-dry paper, whichever is more appropriate. Take care around the frail parts like fingers, as they knock off quite easily. Although they can be stuck back readily enough it all takes time.

Most of the things you need to model, like flowers, books, swords etc. will be a lot easier than hands, and as you have seen, even they are not too difficult if approached in the right way. About the only thing I ever found impossible was a head, and I got over this problem by using a rubber mould and 'borrowing' the head from a very similar figure. This technique will be described later, but in the meantime, never throw away bits of figures that may come in useful. With the use of cutting equipment heads, hands, baskets etc. may quite easily be cut off one piece and fastened to another.

6
Colouring

Colouring may conveniently be divided into two sections – cold and hot. The type you use largely depends on how elaborate you want to be, how strong a finish is required and whether the piece you are colouring is too large to get in the oven.

The oven-baked colours that are provided by various companies are designed to give a finish about as hard as the original glaze, and are therefore preferable. There are cases however where cold painting is the only practical course, and so plastic enamels will have to be used.

Although the finish will not be as hard as the oven baked paints and glazes, it is, nevertheless, hard enough to resist all but scratching with a sharp object, and is also impervious to damp and changes in temperature. Plastic enamels therefore can still do the job pretty well and will last indefinitely.

In the broadest terms, the more colourful the piece of pottery or porcelain you are working on is, the easier it will be to make the repair invisible, especially when the surface is irregular. Conversely, the most difficult repairs are those on plain white.

There are two reasons for this. Firstly, no piece is ever white. If it were possible to paint on white paint straight out of the tin, the job would be a thousand times easier, but when you do this, even on the whitest of white pottery, it stands out like whitewash on a cement wall! The pottery that appeared to be snow white is always grey, blue, brown, green or some other shade, and unless you are very lucky, the matching shade will probably take a fair amount of experimentation and the patience of a yogi.

About the hardest of all things to disguise is a glue joint across the centre of a plain white plate, and as everything is a lot easier, it might be as well to start off with the hardest.

Apart from the difficulty of obtaining the right shade of white, it is usually necessary to paint the whole plate, which rather detracts from its originality. The reason for this is the glaze, which may be likened to a thin piece of glass on top of the pottery. Just like a piece of glass that has been broken, you may stick it back together easily enough but the join always shows, just the same as paint would show if you applied it to the top of a glass panel to match up with the same colour underneath.

If you were to mix exactly the right shade, and paint a stripe over the joint, it may not show from directly above, but it will if viewed from an angle because the glaze forms a clear gap between the paint and the pottery. To paint the entire plate, the use of a brush is not practical as over such a large area it will probably leave marks, so you are left with the alternative of using an 'air brush', which may be justifiable if you take up restoring professionally, but is a large expense for a hobby.

Without wishing to sound defeatist, and after considerable effort to overcome this problem, I ended up of the opinion that on plain white surfaces of any area, like plates, the best thing to do was to glue it together really well, clean off the surplus, and leave it at that. A good repair will only show up as a hairline crack, and this is vastly preferable to a plate in two halves, or cemented up with those ghastly staples they used to use.

Now we come on to the vast range of pottery and porcelain with multi-coloured, varying surfaces where your final result should blend in so well that it takes a close scrutiny with a magnifying glass to find it.

Colour blending is a subject in its own right, and I have to admit that after reading a book on the subject I ended up little the wiser. Fortunately firms like Floquil make such a vast range of colours that normally you will only need to darken or lighten slightly to obtain the colour you want.

The only colours to my knowledge you cannot get in plastic enamels, are the deep translucent blue of the type used on some Royal Doulton pottery, also on Derby, Sèvres and some oriental pieces. The other is turquoise.

For the blue, which incidently is readily available if you use the oven-baked paints, you have two choices. A tube of artists' acrylic paint called Monastel Blue, which might sometimes need the addition of a touch of black or red, also in acrylics, will usually produce the required colour. As this type of paint dries with a matt finish, two or three thin coats of polyurethane varnish will be needed to give it a gloss.

Always have the patience to build up paint and varnish in thin coats, to avoid brush marks and adjust the shade if necessary.

Another alternative for this particular blue can be found in the Enamelcraft cold-enamelling kit. This can be mixed with the very hard clear glaze to give excellent results. We will be going further into the benefits of Enamelcraft when we come on to the restoration of Cloisonné enamels.

Turquoise poster paint is readily available, but you may also use sea green, and if you mix this with a little blue or white as required (the plastic enamels mix quite well with the poster colour) you can achieve most shades of turquoise.

A short time spent in experimenting will pay dividends. This will show you how the paint feels to apply, and how far a small quantity goes. If you have a large area to paint, there is always the problem of how much to mix. If you mix too much, it might go hard before you can use it all. If, half way through the job you feel this happening and add some turpentine to arrest the drying process, the turpentine will tend to lighten the colour by half a shade. If, on the other hand, you mix up less with the intention of mixing another lot later, will you be able to get exactly the same shade twice?

Although the hints in this chapter should enable you to avoid a lot of the pitfalls, only practice will bring about ease and familiarity.

Presuming that you have the piece in front of you that you are going to paint, and a tin of plastic enamel as near as possible in colour, plus a tin of black for darkening and white for lightening as necessary, here is the procedure. Spoon a small quantity of paint out of the tin with your brush on to the mixing palette, closing the lid of the paint as soon as possible. Then, making sure you clean your brush first, spoon out an even smaller quantity of the shading colour. This gives you two puddles of different coloured paint to work from. Now, instead of mixing them together, make another puddle of the mixture you want, drawing on the original puddles for supply. You will probably think this all sounds a bit finicky, but believe me, it can save an awful lot of time. The reason for this is that once you have gone darker than the shade you want, it is almost impossible to lighten it and retain the right colour. If you mixed the first two puddles together and were lucky enough to end up with the right shade immediately you would be extremely lucky. If you failed, the paint would be wasted and you would have to start again.

Caution, and once again patience, are needed. Shades of paint have to be arrived at gradually, so be prepared to add the black or white or whichever shading colour you are using in tiny quantities, and in this way you will not go beyond the point of no return.

Another advantage of using this system of mixing is that it avoids the danger of getting careless and dipping a dirty brush in to a different coloured tin of paint and polluting it.

While you are working, keep a little pot of turpentine and a few tissues handy. Apart from brush cleaning and thinning down the paint, these will be useful for wiping unwanted paint off the pottery. The reason the unwanted paint gets on to the pottery is that when you think you have achieved the right shade, the only way to check is to put a dab on to the surface of the piece. If it matches well, it should blend in to the background so well that you should hardly be able to see it. For the first few checks, you will probably find that your dab of paint sticks out like a sore thumb. This will be for one of two reasons, either it is too light or too dark, so keep modifying with the shading colour and re-checking until you are satisfied. The experimental dabs of paint wipe off easily with a turpentine-dampened tissue.

To say that is all there is to it makes it sound easy, and from the skill point of view it is, again, patience rather than skill is what is needed. Later on, when skill comes with practice, you may be able to speed up a little, but at first, time and care is the answer.

When you have the correct shade of paint, you are ready to cover up your repair. Always apply the paint in thin layers so that the finished job does not stand too proud, and when you have covered the required area, dry the brush on a tissue and go round the edge again spreading the paint a bit further to avoid ending up with a definite edge.

With practice, a lot of different effects can be achieved. The skillful and meagre use of turpentine can make one colour merge into another. This is especially useful on pottery where there are no definite boundaries. The turpentine should be used very sparingly though or it will remove the paint altogether.

Remember that with colours that look white, subtle additions of grey, blue, green or even brown will be needed to achieve a good match. Whites are without doubt the most difficult, and on a few repairs it will be possible to cheat a little by extending the existing pattern over the repair. It may be necessary to balance this up on the opposite side of the pattern to make it look natural. Where you can do this without making it look obvious a lot of time can be saved.

On pieces where a high gloss is needed, the polyurethane varnish will normally darken the paint very slightly. In this case it may well be necessary to put a dab of varnish over the experimental dab of paint (a tiny dab will dry very quickly) to determine how much of a darkening effect it will have. Unfortunately there is no set rule here as different colours are affected more than others.

At the risk of being repetitive, bear in mind that paint will emphasize any imperfections in your preparation, in fact, a lot of imperfections never show up until you paint over them. It is no use thinking a thick layer of paint will cover up the trouble. I have often wished it would, but it will not, so wipe off the paint and put it right.

Make sure your painting, and drying, is done in a dust free place. It only takes a wag of a dog's tail, or someone to walk by on a dusty carpet to give your work a rough finish.

A BRIEF SUMMING UP ON PAINTING

Later on in this book, when we come to the use of the more advanced materials, we will be discussing tools like the artist's air brush for paint-spraying, but the basic principles of colour mixing and application remain the same. Little by little is the key to this job, and that includes painting.

Build up your colours slowly, in thin layers, made thinner by adding a small quantity of turpentine if necessary and letting each one dry before applying the next. Always start on the light side. It is always easier to darken a colour than lighten it.

Some pottery and porcelain has a matt finish. There are two ways of combating this problem, the easiest being a matt varnish obtained in art supply stores. A final coat of this varnish usually achieves the desired result, but in obstinate cases where the surface is almost abrasive, more powder has to be added. This can be anything from talcum powder to fine sand depending on the surface required. Matt paints are only ordinary paints with grit added, and usually this sinks to the bottom of the tin, so always remember to stir well immediately before application.

For restorers who find they need an even harder glaze than polyurethane varnish, but do not wish to use oven-baked glazes, or where the piece is too large for the oven, you may obtain from many of the mail-order suppliers listed in the Appendix a two-part glaze that sets to an extremely hard finish.

Plastic-enamel paints and varnishes eventually set very hard indeed. Although they appear to dry off in a few minutes, it takes a lot longer for them to harden completely – up to six weeks in some cases. Because of this I always tell my customers not to handle the repair for as long as possible. Even a few days after painting it is quite possible to put a finger print in it. There is a lot of difference between touch dry and completely dry.

Because you are applying paint in thin layers they are often a little translucent, so if enough coats are not applied the repair may be faintly visible through the paint. One way to avoid this is to do a base layer of white paint and then build the required colour on top. This method also has the dual advantage of showing up any defects in the repair before you go to the lengths of mixing the correct shade.

Oven-Baked Paints. Many different manufacturers who, as I mentioned earlier, are very aware of the restorers' needs, have brought out a range of pigments which are translucent, and an opacifier which may either be used to make the pigments opaque, or as a white colour in its own right.

Six of these are to be found in the Make-or-break kit together with ceramic putty, epoxy-resin glue, thinners, paint brush and knife, which makes it a very comprehensive kit for a restorer. The pigments are red, blue, green, black, yellow and brown, which together with the white opacifier can be used to produce almost any colour. A colour mixing chart is also included.

Naturally, oven baking is preferable to cold painting, because the finish is as hard as the real thing and therefore makes a more professional repair. Until these low temperature glazes were produced, firing or baking, as you prefer, used to mean the use of a potters kiln. Apart from being very costly to buy, there was always the risk of damage to the pottery due to the very high temperatures used.

The modern glazes are designed to cure at domestic oven temperatures. They only need half an hour at 325 degrees Fahrenheit, which is below the danger level at which some porcelain may discolour. As with the use of Sylmasta, described earlier, the piece should be put in a cold oven, and five minutes allowed for it to reached the required temperature. Also, as pottery and porcelain should never be cooled too quickly, ten or preferably fifteen minutes should be allowed after switching off before opening the oven door. Be very careful to use a heat-proof oven glove, and to place the fired object on to a surface that it will not harm. Pottery holds its heat for quite a while, so do not make a grab at it and then have to drop it because it is too hot to hold! I know it sounds obvious, but it can happen when you are in a hurry to get on to the next stage.

As with all these materials, the manufacturers supply comprehensive instructions, and these should be followed closely for guaranteed results.

Basically, as far as mixing is concerned, one type of paint is very much like another. The main difference with these is that they are translucent. Whereas with plastic enamels, the opacifier is already added, with these pigments you add it yourself to the required quantity. Very little is needed to make the pigment opaque. This may seem like extra work, but you now have the great advantage of being able to reproduce any texture from deep translucency to dull matt by varying the proportions of pigment, opacifier and glaze. In many cases, with careful mixing the whole job of covering a repair and glazing can be done at the same time, and completed with just one firing.

The type of repair you are working on, and the finish you require will determine the method you use. In most cases, the opacifier will be needed to cover the repair. Without it, you would be able to see through the translucent pigment and the join or whatever would be visible. There are far too many different textures in pottery and porcelain to explain how to arrive at each one, and quite a lot of practice and experimentation will be needed to attain perfection. A good plan is to make some little tiles, about two inches square out of Sylmaster and try out a few variations.

I make the suggestion that you try out your experiments on Sylmasta tiles, because if you intend to oven-bake your repairs, it will be Sylmasta, or the putty provided in the make-or-break kit, which can be used exactly the same way, that you will be painting on.

Presuming you have at least five practice-tiles, try out the following combinations. On tile one, just paint on a small quantity of pigment. On tile two, mix a tiny quantity of opacifier with the pigment. On tile three mix some glaze but no opacifier with the pigment. On number four, mix pigment, a small amount of opacifier and some glaze. Lastly, the same as tile four, but more glaze.

Fire all these tiles according to the instructions, and you have a range of textures from dull matt to a fairly deep gloss. The beauty of this material is that having completed the firing, there is no disadvantage adding more glaze and firing again, so in the case of tile three for example, which will be a translucent gloss more glaze and another firing will give it a really deep translucency. Some pottery has its final firing with a really deep glaze, and you can add one or more coats until the right depth is achieved.

The pigment will dry on its own, but firing makes it

stronger. For some restoring jobs, where no surface strength is required, like in the case of a seldom handled ornament, pigment on its own, once fired will suffice. Naturally, the real strength, as with pottery, is in the glaze. Apart from Wedgwood, very few pieces of pottery are matt finish, so in the majority of repairs you will be mixing in glaze, and or adding it on a second firing. This will give great strength to surface abrasion. So much so, in fact, that the manufacturers recommend it for painting monograms and suchlike on plain china dinner services where it will have to withstand the onslaught of knives and forks wielded by hungry eaters, not to mention washing-up scourers, etc!

Try not to be put off by the small amount of extra work involved with adding opacifiers and firing, there is really nothing to it once you have had a little practice, and your end results will be much stronger and far more professional. In most cases, applying the pigments, opacifier and glaze can be accomplished by brush, but if you wish to cover a large area, they can be used in an airbrush with good results, although it may be necessary to thin the glaze down with the thinners provided.

Thinners, it should not be forgotten, may also be used to add to the glaze when applying with a brush for a very thin-effect. Do not make it too thin though; two parts glaze to one part thinner is the limit.

After work, use the thinners to clean brushes and things you have spilled spots of paint on, and you will then be ready for a clean start. Make sure the brush is really clean, by soaking it in the thinners, wiping it on a tissue and then repeating the process until you are sure. A quickly or carelessly cleaned brush is usually a wasted one, and while one brush may be no great loss, it can get expensive to buy a new one too often.

7
Reproducing Patterns

There are a lot of factors to your advantage in this business, not the least being that most patterns used on pottery and porcelain are a series of repetitions, and geometrically regular, so if part of a vase or plate is missing and has to be replaced, you nearly always have something to copy from.

Before the pattern is added, of course, the base colour has to be right. If you are doing the job cold, make sure this coat is completely dry. If you are using the oven-baked pigments, this coat can be fired, the pattern added, and then depending whether the pattern is under the glaze or, like a lot of oriental pottery, on top of it, you may need to put a final glaze on and fire again.

Unlike a polyurethane varnish, the glaze supplied in the make-or-break kit is completely colourless, and so you will not be making the area a shade darker each time you re-glaze and refire. This is why the finish can be so much more exact for texture and colour.

Now for the pattern. Some people can look at a pattern and then nonchalently reproduce the whole thing. I wish I could, it would save a lot of time, but freehand art of any kind is beyond me, and if I try I usually end up with one squiggle too few or too many where my pattern and the original pattern meet up.

If you have the same trouble, there are one or two ways of getting round it, the first of which I shall call the 'semi-freehand'.

It is by no means unusual for a pattern to have a key feature. This key may take the form of a circle, an arc, a bold line among lighter lines etc. The important thing is that you can sort out one easily reproduced part of the pattern, and taking care with your dividers to measure the correct intervals, superimpose it over the repaired section.

Provided your measurements are correct, your key line or shape should occur at regular intervals across the blank repair, ending up in exactly the right place to join up with the original pattern. It is worth stressing that great care is needed to get the measurements really accurate, or it is quite likely that your new pattern will either overlap the original or be too high or low.

One good way to obviate this is to make little dots of pigment where the top and bottom of your key should appear. Make these in the same colour as the pattern so they become invisible as you build it up. Having got your key feature evenly spaced and marked in, it is now a lot easier to reproduce the rest of the pattern around it.

If you are using the fired pigments, it can be quite a help to mark the top and bottom extremities of the pattern by sticking on a border of tape. This can be done on plastic enamels if they are really dry, but if not, the tape may pull some of the paint up on removal.

When using this method, beware of altering curves. Only on straight sided cylindrical vases can you be sure that your

Figs. 11, 12. Reproducing a pattern (*left*) incorrect and (*right*) correct

taped borders are accurate. On trumpet and other shapes the tape tends to take the shortest line between the two ends of the original pattern. To a certain extent this inconvenience can be allowed for, but on some shapes it is best to use dots of pigment to make out the border.

Your dividers are capable of giving you every measurement you need, so make full use of them. They can give you not only the correct distance between sections of the pattern but also the dimensions of each individual part of the pattern and the distance between it and the edge of the pottery.

The type of dividers available from stationary shops are quite suitable, but make sure you blunt down the points on a stone to avoid scratching. All dividers are, of course, are two arms, hinged at one end tightly enough to retain the angle you set them at. With two thin pieces of wood, each pointed at one end, and hinged with a small nut and bolt at the other, it is the work of a few minutes to make your own. Wooden dividers have the dual advantage of not scratching the pottery or the repair, and the ability to retain a dab of pigment on the tip so you can measure and mark out at the same time. This can also be done with the steel type by strapping a couple of sharpened matchsticks or cocktail sticks on to the tips with tape, and saves you the trouble of holding dividers in one hand and a paint brush in the other to mark with.

Patterns are not half so daunting as they sometimes look. Fortunately most breakages occur near the edge of things where there are clear boundaries to work from. Like nearly everything else in this job, the building up of patterns can be done in easy stages, only needing care and patience. With a well-matched, fired-on texture and an accurate reproduction of the pattern followed by another light glazing and re-firing, you will be quite staggered at times to find how difficult it can be to find the repair. Even when you know where it is!

8
Advanced Materials and Techniques

It is possible to buy very sophisticated cutting and drilling equipment — it is like making the choice between a Volkswagen or a Rolls. They will both get you from A to B; the real choice lies in how much you want to spend.

So far in this book, your total outlay could be kept under ten dollars, an incredibly small amount compared to the value of some of the pieces you may work on.

The tools mentioned in this section are only necessary for the more complicated repairs, but even so, I have kept the price down to a minimum. The Rolls buyer may well go out and buy a diamond edged cutting saw and grinding wheels, and a powerful electric motor to drive them. Very nice too, if you

12. A flexible drive and grinding wheels

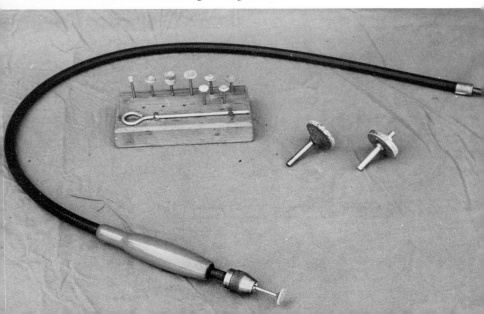

13. A drill with a stone-cutting wheel

have a few hundred dollars to spare. I am a Volkswagen man myself, and I have found that cutting and grinding can be done equally well and effectively with a three-eighth electric drill of the type available at tool shops, a selection of carborundum grinding-wheels, a stand, a stone cutting disc and a flexible drive.

Even if you buy the most modern, four-speed drill the total cost should be under fifty dollars. If you already have a smaller quarter-inch drill, this will most likely be adequate, I just happened to have the larger type. The larger the motor, of course, the harder it can work without wearing out. Also, most of the larger drills have a variable speed gearbox which can be useful for certain jobs.

Many of the grinding jobs can only be done with the use of a flexible drive, which can be held rather like a pen, and therefore used quite accurately. This sort of control would be impossible with a heavy drill in your hands.

While using the flexible drive, which incidentally is available from any good hardware store, it is convenient to have the drill mounted in a stand. This is not essential, but if it is not held down, the drill tends to jump around a bit. It also has a chuck revolving at high speed which could cause injury to clothing or flesh. If you do not have a stand, I would suggest you work at floor level with the drill confined to a carboard box left open at the top for cooling air to reach it. In this way you can work in safety and stop the drill from working its way to the edge of a table and falling off.

A selection of the kind of miniature grinding wheels you will need is shown in photograph 12. The different shapes all have their uses as you will find. A good tool shop will either stock them or be able to obtain them for you.

The stone cutting wheel, (photograph 13) is usually sold without a centre, or arbor as I believe they call it in the trade. This is presumably so that you can buy a centre appropriate to your drill. The separate centre will most likely be a sloppy fit in the cutting wheel with two large washers for clamping. Centre this carefully with plenty of Araldite in the middle and clamp it together, and you now have a permanent shaft to fit the stone cutter to the drill chuck. This is how I fastened my wheel about five years ago, and the centre is still as solid as a rock.

One other necessary item is a couple of drills, of the type that are used for drilling glass. These should be as small as possible, as their main use is for inserting wire dowels to hold limbs in place when restoring figurines.

Before we come on to the practical use of these tools, a

word of warning. In nearly every case they will be revolving at high speed, and frequently causing particles of hot, hard pottery to fly off. Should one of these nasty chunks find some delicate spot like your eye, it could cause a painful injury at the least, and permanent blindness at the worst!! Please, when using power tools, wear goggles. Mostly you will only raise a cloud of dust, and apart from the fact that this will not do your eyes any good either, do not be misled, the hard chunks might only fly off occasionally, but it only needs one. It is too big a price to pay for carelessness.

Now return to the practical side of restoring. You will remember in the chapter on gluing I mentioned the case where a piece of pottery or porcelain 'springs' when it breaks, and will not quite go‾ back together again. The result is, that however hard you try to get the gluing accurate, you end up with a step at some part of the join.

Exactly the same thing happens with a badly aligned joint, occasionally, however careful you are, a piece will just not go together well for one reason or another, or else it slips out of position before the glue dries and this goes unnoticed.

Whatever the reason, the step is a bit of an embarrassment. It is usually quite noticeable to the eye, and even more so to the touch, and is best ground off.

Grinding, even with power tools, is quite a slow business, and should be treated as such. A light, firm touch is ideal, letting the carborundum wheel do the work. Some pottery is quite soft once the hard glaze is penetrated, and if you are too impatient and press too hard, you might grind away too much. Tend to be over cautious if anything.

Hold the flexible drive firmly, if you were to allow it to ride up out of the section you are grinding it could damage some other part of the pottery – or you! Having a fast, rotary action, the wheel will naturally try to roll in the direction it is turning – the harder you press, the harder it will try.

If, on the other hand you hold it too lightly, it will tend to bounce. Apart from damaging the wheel, this will probably knock little chunks out of the pottery as well.

Try out your first bit of grinding on an expendable piece of pottery if possible, and you will soon get to know the pressure required.

When you come to grind off the step, use one of the blunt edged wheels. A small wheel of about $\frac{1}{2}$ inch diameter copes with the normal step, which is likely to be less than 1/32 inch in height. For more extreme cases, like a very large vase, where the step may be more like $\frac{1}{8}$ inch or larger, a 2 inch wheel will be more suitable.

The important thing is to grind the area flat. True, if you make a few unnecessary indentations or troughs, they can be filled up again with quick-setting plastic or Sylmasta, but all this takes more time, and with care, it is quite easy to grind the pottery nice and flat in the first place.

Depending on the height of the step, you will have to grind back half-an-inch or more to get a nice level. Your sense of touch is the best thing to tell you when you have achieved it. Check often to make sure you do not go too far.

Remember that you will have a corresponding step on the reverse side of the piece. In some cases you may be able to get away with this one, the inside of a vase for instance where it is not visible or alternatively if the piece is your own, and you can not be bothered to do the back.

If you have to do it, this side may need the low side filling rather than the high side grinding, especially on fairly thin objects, to keep the strength. In this case, the glaze will need

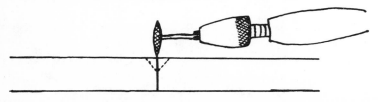

Fig. 13. Grinding out a join with a small conical wheel

scoring with the grinding wheel to make the filler adhere properly.

Using the low-temperature glaze described, once you have ground the area nice and flat, all you should now have to do is to mix the necessary pigment and/or opacifier with the glaze and fire it, and this should make the join neatly disappear.

On some items, like the head on a small figurine, it may be very difficult or even impossible to apply pressure while the glue is curing. Alternatively, the tape, or whatever the pressure is being applied with may slip or break. The result may not put the piece out of alignment and make a step, but it may mean that the glue joint is not really tight.

If it has come apart enough to lose its strength, you will probably do best to take it apart as already described and start again. In some cases however, the joint will be tight enough for strength, but paint will seek out any hollows in the joint and make them stand out. Usually, and most annoyingly, these hollows are too thin to press in quick or slow setting plastic, and as I have already said, paint, for some unknown reason will never fill this kind of gap up. The answer therefore is to widen the gap so that filler may be applied, and to do this, you need one of the sharp edged grinding wheels to 'V' it out (*see* fig. 13).

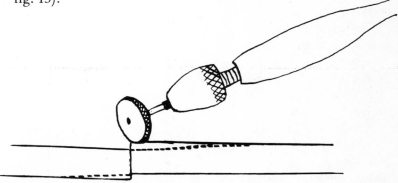

Fig. 14. Grinding a surface down flat with a blunt-edged wheel

For all places that are awkward to get at with $\frac{1}{2}$ inch wheels, use the tiny conical wheel. I have always found this one most useful for inaccessible places like armpits on small figures, whether to grind off pottery, or filler that you can not get at with a file or wet-and-dry paper.

As pottery and porcelain, especially the latter, is extremely hard, the small grinding wheels do not last very long, and soon tend to go oval. When this happens, throw them away and replace them, or they start to bounce and do damage. They are very inexpensive and the cost is easily absorbed in the price of a repair.

Carborundum wheels are quite adequate for opening up a crack, or smoothing off a small step, but they take a long time to cut right through a piece of pottery. For this job you need a stone cutting wheel.

This is a disc about 9 inches in diameter and looks a bit like hardboard, so much so, that you would not think it would cut butter, and yet it goes through thick pottery with very little trouble. The secret of its efficiency lies in the fact that it is embedded with diamond chippings. Strangely enough, if you happen to touch it with your hand by mistake, even when it is revolving at high speed, it will only give you a friction burn! Unpleasant, but surprisingly lenient compared to the way it cuts harder materials.

To use this wheel, you will need to mount the drill in a stand. Preferably, this should be screwed down on to a bench, or a piece of wood large enough to keep it firm while in use.

Pottery, as I have said, it will cope with easily. Porcelain is much harder, but this only means the wheel will take slightly longer to cut through it.

While using the stone-cutting wheel, like the carborundum wheels, use goggles of some kind. At the very least, the ensuing dust cloud will cover you and everything else in range. Dust can easily be cleaned off everything else but your eyes. Some particles are larger than others, and often red hot.

If you ever try any grinding in the dark, you will see the pottery glowing with heat, and little particles flying off like sparks.

I know I keep harping on the safety angle, but believe me, the danger is very real. The nature of what you are doing usually means that you are staring at the spot you are grinding, and more often than not your eyes are right in the firing line.

The stone cutter is most often used for cutting off the broken top of a vase. It often happens that a vase top is so

CUT HERE

Fig. 15. A vase with a broken neck, suitable for conversion into a lamp

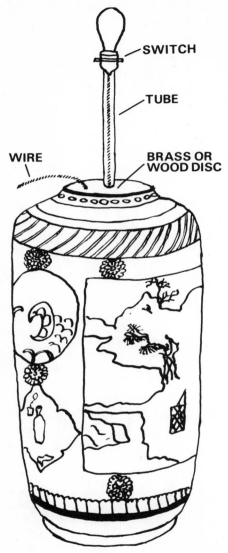

SWITCH

TUBE

WIRE

BRASS OR WOOD DISC

Fig. 16. The broken vase converted

badly damaged that repair is only worthwhile if it is a matter of great importance to a customer to have it restored to the original shape.

Where you make the cut depends on three things, the extent of the damage, the pattern and the shape. Obviously it has to be cut below the lowest area of damage, but the pattern and the shape often determine just how much lower. You would not make the cut half way through a patterned panel, for instance, if just below the pattern was a line which would be suitable for the top of the cut vase.

Some Oriental vases have tops like ginger jars and some are trumpet shaped, but when cut off at the shoulder look just the authentic ginger jar type. In this case, and it happens more frequently than you would suppose, it is often possible to cut off the broken top, round off the edge with a carborundum wheel, re-glaze it or gild it as the case may be, and end up with a modified but near perfect vase, a suitable ornament in its own right.

Another way of turning a similarly damaged vase into a useful proposition is to make it into a lamp. The procedure is as before, but instead of rounding off the newly cut edge, make a brass or black (ebonized) wood disc, fit an extension brass tube, tightly glued in to a hole in the centre of the disc, and make it into a lamp.

The height of the extension tube depends on the size of shade you require, in some cases a tube might not even be necessary. Make sure either the hole in the disc, or the internal diameter of the tube if you are using one, are the right size for the light fitting. Your local electrician will show you the fittings and the screw in pillars that will attach them to the disc or tube.

If you already happen to have a brass tube in your oddments box, but it is too big for the light fitting, don't worry, it can easily be set in with some quick setting plastic. If you think you might ever want to unscrew it, put some grease on the

14. A vase with the top cut off to be made into a lamp

thread before setting it in the plastic and it will unscrew whenever you want.

Some people like a hole drilled in the base or in the side of a vase to take the wire. Personally I would advise against this. Funny enough, it is a quirk of the trade, that a really well made lamp, even if the neck has been cut off, is worth very little less than the complete vase would be, but cut a hole in the side or the base and the value is lowered immediately.

It is quite easy to drill a small hole in the disc, and feed the wire down through this and up through the tube, (before sticking the disc on!!) as in the diagram. The switch can either be in the light fitting, the wire, or there is also a push button type you can fit into the disc. Again, your electrician will be able to advise.

Most department stores sell lamp shades, or preferably just the frames, so you can select your own material to match the vase.

15. An airbrush

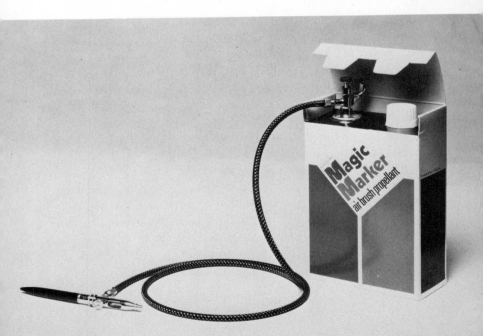

Finally, take very good care to cut the neck off straight, a clear circle drawn with a Magic Marker makes a good guide. Pause frequently to check, and make sure you are holding the vase level so that the underneath edge is also following the line. With a vase of any diameter it is best to keep turning as you are cutting so that the wheel is not allowed to travel too far in. If it did, and you were to move for some reason you might snap the wheel or break the vase, so as usual, take it steadily, hold on firmly and let the wheel do the work.

Used with great care, the stone-cutting wheel can also do more delicate tasks of the type normally reserved for your grinding wheels. On occasions, large areas of pottery can be skimmed off quite quickly by using (lightly) the flat face of the wheel. Do be careful though, that you do not take too much off, which is easily done. Also, if you use the flat-face of the wheel, you could easily break it by pressing too hard.

Finally, when grinding with the stone cutting wheel or the carborundum wheels, try and get used to the system of frequently checking your progress rather than bending over close to the grinding area with your face. These wheels have been known to break up if you press too hard and get them too hot. This has yet to happen to me, but if it did, large chunks of hot matter are likely to be flying round at speed.

If you can do the grinding jobs outside, so much the better, the dust, as I have said, rises like a desert sandstorm and leaves a liberal coating over everything in sight.

The last of the most costly items you may need is a rather delightful little gadget called an airbrush. This is nothing more than a miniature paint sprayer about the same size as a large fountain pen. It may be worked by an aerosol can of propellant, or a foot pump. The main advantage of spraying is that a thinner and more even coat may be applied than with a brush. This can be especially useful when a large area has to be covered in a single colour.

An airbrush is quite easy to use, and all the paint we have

discussed so far will go through it, some admittedly more easily than others. In some cases it will be necessary to thin the paint down, but this is no disadvantage, as more thin coats always look better than fewer thick ones.

When spraying a decorated item, bear in mind that the spray will tend to cover up the pattern as well as the part you want it to cover. This is best masked off prior to painting when possible, and this can be accomplished by painting a thin coat of wax on the pattern before spraying (wax polish, warmed up is quite adequate). This can then be washed off when the paint is nice and dry, and before the glaze is applied.

Matt colours may be used, but you will probably experience difficulty at first getting the right consistency. Practice however will produce dividends here, because it is a very good way of achieving the very difficult Wedgwood jasper-ware textures.

Meticulous care is needed to clean out the nozzles both after painting and in between colour changes, but then just the same care is needed with brushes for continued good results.

If you want to see an airbrush in action before spending your money, most photographic retouching studios and graphic art studios use them. Although people at these studios are usually very busy, they are also mostly extremely helpful, and at a time convenient to them, would no doubt arrange a small demonstration.

Useful though this may be, practice is the only way really to get used to using this sort of equipment. Tell yourself that there is nothing you cannot do if you try, and soon you will be doing it without thinking anything of it.

9
Advanced Moulding

Whereas plasticene or plaster of paris is adequate for moulding simple items, nine times out of ten there are a few imperfections that need repairing or filling before the job can be called complete.

On simple shapes that can easily be got at this is no great problem, just a bit of a nuisance.

There is another problem of the rigid mould, that of the undercut. Just to explain this rather pretentious and suspiciously technical sounding little word, let us take the example of making a mould of an egg. In two moulds, there is no problem, the moulds can simply be lifted off with no harm done. Just suppose, on the other hand, that you wanted a one piece mould of three quarters of an egg. Then, with the rigid mould, you have a problem, you have gone past the point of maximum diameter, and you cannot remove the mould without stretching the lower section to that diameter.

This is an undercut, and the only ways of getting over the problem are two part or multiple moulds, or a flexible mould that can be stretched and then return to the right shape and size without damage.

I chose an egg for the example, because the same problems occur with moulding a head, a quite similar shape. Many would consider, of course. that if a figure has lost its head the only answer is to throw it away, because its identity will have been completely stripped. To judge by some of the efforts I have seen to build a new head, I would tend to agree. Pottery and porcelain figures are either moulded, or made by expert sculptors. The head is the most difficult part of all, and is not, in my opinion, worth attempting to make unless you are yourself an expert.

With moulding, the picture is entirely different. With a lot of figures, there is a duplicate around, in fact, with moulded figures there may be thousands. If a duplicate is not to be found, there will be lots of very similar figures whose heads would not look out of place if used on the broken figure. There are also many examples of a piece comprising two or more figures, where a head moulded from another in the group would be identical, cupids for instance.

The material used for making these moulds is Adrub RTV which is a rubber mould compound marketed by Adhesive Products Corp., whose address may be found with the other manufacturers at the back of the book. RTV silicone also may be used.

Rubber moulds are very easy to make and use, they are available as a single component to be squeezed straight out of a tube in to the mould box, or as a two part mixture which is probably more suitable for pouring, being more liquid.

Both types cure at room temperature, the one-pack tube in about eight hours, and the two-pack again having the advantage in that you can make a stronger mixture that will cure in as little as twenty minutes. For maximum detail, Adrub RTV is recommended, but full details are available from Adhesive Products Corp. if you want to make your own choice.

When they are cured, these rubber moulds are very flexible, especially if their thickness is kept down to a quarter of an inch or less, so they can be pulled off without damage or distortion. They should not be made thicker than half an inch if possible. The motto is 'the thinner the better' for both curing and flexibility. Moulds of half an inch or over will need forty-eight hours or more to cure.

The first task is to make a 'mould box'. Plasticene is as good as anything for this, and still using a head as an example, the box can be built up from the shoulders of the figure you are taking the mould from. The easiest way is to roll out the plasticene flat on the table in an oblong and then join the two ends together to form a cylinder that, when placed on the shoulders, will give the head about $\frac{1}{8}$ inch clearance around and $\frac{1}{4}$ inch on top. Pinch the lower end in to the shoulders so the moulding liquid will not run out, and there you have it.

Now pour the Adrub slowly into the box over the head, allowing time for each little pouring to settle. If you poured the whole lot in at once, you may well get air bubbles trapped under the chin, ears or nose, which will give the finished mould imperfections in the surface. Use a slow trickle only, around and around the gap between the head and the plasticene.

When the mould box is full, just leave it to set for the required time. Presuming this time has passed, no trouble should be experienced in peeling off the plasticene box. If it is a bit obstinate though, carefully cut it away from the Adrub with your razor knife, taking care not to go through the mould.

With the plasticene removed, the Adrub can be pulled off the head. The thinner you managed to make it, the easier it can be removed, but it should be quite flexible and give no trouble. The only thing that might stop it from coming off easily is if the bottom of your box, around the chin and neck was too wide, and you now have a big wad around there that will not stretch easily. In this case, cut off enough of the surplus to make it easy.

For the occasional time when a two part mould is required, supposing you are still moulding a head, the obvious procedure would be to lay the head on its side, and make the box accordingly so that the Adrub came half way up the side of the nose, and then turn it over and do the same again.

Where a two part mould is going to be made one part on top of another, without removing the first part, a smear of petroleum jelly will be needed where the join is, because although Adrub will not stick to a surface like porcelain, it will stick to itself, so the Vaseline will ensure that the two halves part easily.

Although it applies to almost every stage of restoration, it is probably worth mentioning that a mould will only be as good as the moulding surface, so make sure that it is spotlessly clean before you start.

Now you have the completed mould, the only thing left to do is make the head, and this entails nothing more complicated than mixing up some Araldite, enough to fill the mould, and leaving it overnight to set.

Your newly made head now needs fitting to the figure, and this is done by methods already described. It will probably need cutting or filing to fit the figure before it can be stuck on with some more Araldite. When this join has been made good, the decorating, glazing and firing can be done with the make-or-break kit materials, and it will now be impossible for anyone without an infra-red light to tell it from a perfect figure.

Used properly and strictly by the manufacturers recommendations, these moulds can give a really superb and accurate replica, and restore a large part of the value to what was once considered only fit for the dustbin.

Rubber materials do no damage whatsoever to the piece used for moulding, only you can damage the piece by careless handling, so if care is taken a piece borrowed for a pattern can be returned in perfect condition.

10

Restoring Cloisonné and Champlevé Enamels

Cloisonné and champlevé enamels come under the heading of Oriental. In actual fact, both originated in France, hence the very French sounding names. The Chinese, however were manufacturing both by the early part of the fifteenth century, and still do so to this day. At the height of the European craze for Oriental ware in the nineteenth century, the ever enterprising Japanese also started making cloisonné, and outdid the Chinese for intricacy of decoration.

Whereas the Chinese kept mostly to simple patterns, flowers and basic animals, the Japanese produced incredibly delicate butterfly and floral designs, which makes it quite easy to tell the two apart.

Cloisonné is basically a metal base, usually copper, in the form of a vase, plate etc., with a series of fine wires soldered on in the early examples, and stuck on later, forming patterns. The little reservoirs or cloisons in between the wires are then filled with different coloured enamels and then fired, during which process the enamel is fused to the metal.

In the later, Japanese examples, the surface is then polished smooth and glazed, and the result, in both cases is very beautiful.

Champlevé is made by a different process, the base, which is usually brass, is much heavier, and the pattern is scooped out. The resulting troughs are then filled with enamel and the piece is fired.

Enamel is a kind of glass, coloured with the same sort of

metallic oxides used to colour pottery glazes. The surface is very similar, and in a lot of cases, similar techniques can be used for repair.

As cloisonné is far more delicate, both in strength and design, it is correspondingly vulnerable to damage, and repairs tend to be far more complex than champlevé, so we shall take the easy way out and leave it until last, so you can have the maximum possible amount of practice on other things first.

Champlevé Repairs. Unlike pottery, porcelain and cloisonné, champlevé can usually be dropped on to something hard, and suffer very little damage as a result. The usual thing being a dent or bits of enamel chipped out.

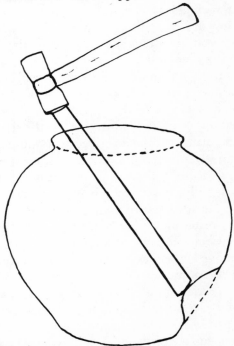

Fig. 17. Beating out a dent in a champlevé pot

In the case of a dent, depending on the size and depth, you may have a small panel beating job on your hands. I say 'may', because unless you can get at the back of the dent easily, it is often better to fill it from the outside. Indiscriminate bashing is far too liable to do even more damage than you started with. Most vases, for instance, have quite narrow necks, which means that a lot of the time you are working blind. Figure 17 shows one feasible way round this problem providing the neck is wide enough.

The shaft used for the actual point of contact in this diagram is wood, and the outside area around the dent is resting on wood as well. The bronze is usually fairly thick, and does not alter shape easily. To overcome its reluctance, you have to use the hammer with confidence. Take regular looks at the effect you are achieving. If nothing is happening, which is quite normal, and you are doing no damage to the surrounding area, try hitting a bit harder.

If the bronze is too thick, and the dent will not come out however hard you try, there is another way of assessing the situation; on a vase, it is likely that the dent is not liable ever to be noticed on the inside. In this case, do the repair from the outside in the manner to be described in a minute, and forget about the inside. Sometimes a dent will come out easily, but when the brass is really thick and well creased it would have to be heated with an oxy-acetyline torch, and this would undoubtedly damage the surrounding enamels.

On bowls, plates and other items where the inside of the dent is clearly and annoying visible, and you or your customer wishes it removed at any cost, you will have to be a bit more violent and use a proper metal panel beaters 'dolly'. Panel beaters have a series of dollies of varying curves, and the idea is to pick one nearest in shape to the internal contour of the undamaged part of the champleve.

The striking surface of the dolly is also quite large, so when the dent is restored to its original shape, the metal around it acts as a brake, and you do not end up with a dent bulging outwards instead of inwards.

Quite a lot of force is sometimes necessary, so cushion the outside against a folded blanket or similar for minimum damage.

Do not ever be tempted to do this job with an ordinary hammer, anything short of the correct shaped dolly will result in multiple dents where there was one before.

Dollies can be bought from a garage suppliers, but if you are on good terms with your local garage, they will probably let you borrow one, although they may well ask for a cash deposit. This is fair enough, because most garages have lost a lot of tools this way. I would say that for the rare occasions you come across this kind of repair it is hardly worth purchasing a complete set of dollies, most of which you may never use.

Having knocked out the dent from the inside, the repair now has to be completed from the outside. The knock that caused the dent originally will have also loosened the enamel, which, in turn, will have dropped out. It is most unlikely that any pieces of enamel will have dropped out whole. If they have, of course, they can now be stuck back in place.

Far more likely, you will be presented with the piece to repair with empty troughs where the enamel used to be, in which case, it has to be repaired with quick setting plastic.

If the brass in the empty trough is smooth, it pays to score it with a pointed object to provide a key for the plastic. Press the plastic well in, and fill to just above the surface. On very shallow repairs like this, the plastic may be rubbed down as soon as it is hard, and then decorated.

On the occasions where you decide to leave the dent as it is, and merely fill and repair it from the outside, the same rules apply as with pottery. First make sure the area is clean, dry and grease free. Score the brass, and fill the whole area oversize in layers of $\frac{1}{4}$ inch maximum.

To allow for any shrinkage, it is now best to let well alone for a few hours, so we will assume this time has elapsed and you are about to make a start again.

Take an 8 inch round file, and carefully shape the plastic to the contour of the vase. Bear in mind that the surface you are filing probably curves in more than one direction. It becomes necessary to think three dimensionally on these sort of jobs, and the best way to do this is to frequently inspect from all angles, and make sure you are not filing off too much in any one direction.

When using the round file, do so with a diagonal action. If you were to file to and fro in a straight line you would end up with a furrow, and the idea of using a comparatively long round file at this stage is to take off all the high spots. A flat file is not so suitable at this stage because the blunt edge will not ride smoothly over the inevitable bumps and hillocks left after filling.

Possibly you will prefer to use a half-round file, which has a shallower curve, for this preparatory work. We all develop our own style after a bit of practice, so the choice is a purely personal one. I have always found the round file particularly effective on two way curves.

If you are wondering why all this rather grand-sounding talk about multi-directional curves has suddenly come into the book at this late stage, it is because a lot of champlevé and cloisonné is in the body of a vase or bowl etc., whereas with pottery, filling is usually confined to the lip or edge of the piece and damage to the body is usually a sticking together job.

When you are working at the edge of a piece, the curve is usually straightforward and easy to see. When your work is further down and well away from the guide-line of the edge, the curves can be very deceptive. Two-directional is a false description. What you are doing really is making part of a sphere, so the curve runs in every direction from the highest point. For the sake of your filing, however, you have to take into account the curve you see by looking down from the top as well as the one you see from the side.

This may sound rather obvious, but the fact remains that a lot of people have trouble achieving the right shape on this sort of repair because they do not view the job from *every* angle.

With the long, round file, work towards the correct shape leaving the whole area slightly oversize, and taking care not to scratch the surrounding area. The enamel is pretty scratch proof, but the brass is soft and will mark very easily.

There may well be depressions that will need building up with more filler before this stage is completed, so wipe off the dust, score for a key if smooth and re-fill.

You may need to do this quite a few times the first time you try this sort of repair, because it is so easy to file off the crown of the curve. In view of this, it is often a good idea not to trust your eye at first, and check the curve physically. To do this you need a thin strip of flexible plastic or springy steel preferably as long as about half the circumference of the vase at least. Hold this strip on to the surface with your repair in the middle so that it makes contact all the way along its length. Where it passes over the repair it will now tell you exactly how accurate your curve is. If you have flattened the crown there will be clearance between the strip and the filler, if the crown is too high, on the other hand, the clearance will be on either side of the repair.

Do this check from other angles too, not just nine o'clock to three o'clock, try it from twelve to six, and two to six etc., always with the repair in the middle of the strip, which, in turn, should always pass across the crown of the repair.

By this method, your repair must end up right even if it is quite large in area, so when you are satisfied, smooth it off with wet-and-dry. Do this with a circular motion evenly over the repair so as not to cause any more depressions, and although you are bound to shine up the surrounding brass near the edge, do so as little as possible, as it all makes more work.

When you have completed this stage and washed off the inevitable sludge, you will notice that the area immediately around the repair is a lot brighter than the rest of the piece. This is because the wet-and-dry has scraped off the accumulated grime of ages. It is now decision time. Whereas with pottery, which is usually meant to look beautiful rather than old, it is best to clean the whole piece thoroughly, with champlevé, a lot of people like it to look old.

If the piece is your own, I am in favour of a total clean up job. Grime has no bearing on authenticity, and its removal in my opinion improves the overall image of the ornament. This is, however, only my own viewpoint, you may well feel differently, or more important, your customer might, so it is as well to find out.

While you are doing so, bear in mind that substances such as varnish are often used on champlevé both to make it look a lot older than it really is, and to hide up other damage or earlier bad repairs, so make sure your customer is aware that cleaning may result in more work. If he is happy for you to go ahead, the onus is on him to pay any extra charge for additional work. It is always rather embarrassing to try and explain afterwards why a job cost a lot more than was first thought.

Depending on the decision, the repair must now be decorated to match the surrounding colour, so if you decide to clean, it must be now. The best material used for this purpose is the polish or rubbing compound used to bring the lustre back to a car's paintwork when it has gone a bit dull. It is a lightly abrasive substance similar to but more effective than Brasso, but the latter will do the job.

As well as being slightly abrasive, such polish contains ammonia, which effectively removes all the grease while the abrasive does the shining. The effect, on champlevé, is to lighten and brighten it without scratching. As would wet-and-dry, which would also shine up the brasswork in a garish and distasteful manner.

Champlevé colours are always dull, and this can be reproduced by adding a small amount of talc to the plastic-enamel paint. Even when you have the right texture, however, your base colour will still look cleaner than the surrounding enamel, but do not worry about this for the moment, just make sure the basic colour is the same.

The next stage is to reproduce the brass divisions, and a mixture of your liquid-leaf gold and black will produce the colour. As for the positioning of the divisions, this will be a replica of the surrounding pattern, and following on from it. Champlevé divisions, or the patterns they form are always quite simple and basic. If it will help, mark them out in pencil (lightly) on the base colour, having taken measurements with the dividers.

If you look closely at the surface of champlevé, you will find that it is not only dull but speckled. The whole surface is covered in tiny spots, varying in colour from medium brown to black, and this is now the essential difference between your repair and the rest of the piece.

When I realised that my early repairs were not looking quite right, and eventually found this to be lack of speckle, I tried all sorts of methods to produce it, none of which was very effective. The obvious method of applying spots with the tip of the brush made them either too large, too evenly sized and spaced or took too long.

Like most problems, it resolved itself eventually. A child would no doubt have thought of it sooner, because if you give a child a painting set it is the sort of thing they do naturally.

You will need some practice with this on a piece of scrap paper to get the right consistency and range, but the idea is to mix up some dark brown paint, very much thinned with turps. Use a fairly short, stiff haired brush. It is important that the brush should have a bit of spring. Now get a small quantity of the thinned paint on the end of the brush, and hold it in your left hand about six inches from the target. Then flick the bristles of the brush with the index finger nail of your right hand. The result will be thousands of tiny spots just where you wanted them.

Do practise first though, because by varying the thinness of the paint, the amount on the brush and the distance from the target, you can make quite a difference in the size and quantity of the spots.

This process, which for want of a better name I shall call 'spotting', should complete the repair, and blend it in nicely with the surrounding enamel. If it does not, on this or any other repair, there always has to be a reason, and often a close scrutiny with a magnifying glass to compare your finish with the original is necessary to find out why.

It may be that your base colour was not quite right, and if so, there is not a lot you can do about it at this stage but start again, which is why it is always so very important to get the right base colour before proceeding with the decoration.

Occasionally I have come across champlevé with tiny white dots amongst the brown or black ones, and applying these will then give you the right look. Sometimes the surface is pock-marked with tiny blow holes where the piece was over-fired. This often used to happen when the kiln got a bit too hot, and can be emulated near the beginning of the job, just after applying the filler. This kind of plastic goes through a jelly stage before it hardens, and during this stage, which only lasts for a minute or so, prod holes in it with a pin or needle. Make sure you go deep enough so the holes are still there after you have rubbed the surplus off.

If the surface is still too shiny, a light, and I mean light, rub-over with steel wool will dull it down a bit. If, on the other hand it is too dull, a thinned coat of varnish should do the trick.

There is no reason, with champlevé, why a repair done with care should be visible when complete. On semi-dull, decorative surfaces repairs can be quite easily lost into the surroundings. Only on very flat, high-gloss surfaces is a repair difficult to hide completely.

Before we finish with champlevé, there are two other types of repair I get quite a lot of, namely missing handles and bases.

To deal with the handles first, these usually end in a peg at each end which fits tightly into corresponding holes in the vase. If one or both of these get knocked off or fall off, they can quite easily be stuck back in with an epoxy-resin glue. If you use the same principles in gluing as for pottery, i.e., lots of pressure where possible, having cleaned and de-greased the area first, it will stick just as well as solder, and a lot less noticeably too.

Sometimes, one handle is missing, and this presents a few alternatives, depending mostly on how much you or your customer wishes to spend.

On a very valuable piece, it may be worth having a new handle cast from a mould taken from the existing one. Present day gun metal looks fairly similar. Brass these days, however, looks far lighter in colour, so a casting made out of it would look cheap and nasty. The metal workers who do the job will be able to advise you.

On most pieces with one handle missing I usually take the short cut (with my customer's consent, of course) of removing the remaining handle. A few light taps on each side with a hammer is usually all that is needed. I prefer to get the handle out this way, because a lot of them on similarly sized champlevé vases are the same size, and it is quite likely that the next time you get this repair in, your spare handle might fit. It is always preferable to use the genuine article where possible, and if you hacksaw the handle off you will not be able to use it again.

Having removed the handle, you are now left with two

holes each side to plug with quick setting plastic. After rubbing down and painting, it is most unusual for anyone to be able to find where the holes were.

As a lot of vases do not have handles anyway, this method of repair seldom looks out of place.

Finally, your third alternative is to make a two part rubber mould (a one part mould is sometimes possible if you remove the other handle) and make a new handle out of Araldite. This can then be stuck in position and painted to match the other handle.

Although a strong and life-like replica can be made in this way, some people object to the feel of it. Plastic has a warm and most un-metal like feel that is impossible to disguise.

The base of most champlevé pieces is just a disc which is pressed in or soldered. If you have the original, it is an easy job to stick it back in with epoxy-resin glue. If you have not, and you feel that cutting a disc of brass from a sheet is beyond you, cut out a paper pattern, and take it to your local metalworkers who should be able to make one up very reasonably.

The bases are never made of the heavy-gauge metal the rest of the piece is made of; 1/16 inch is quite common. It will, admittedly look a bit bright to start with, but thinned black paint will soon tone it down again.

Cloisonné Repairs.

Damage to cloisonné is usually more extensive, partly because it is not so robust as champlevé, and partly because the wire often falls out as well as the enamel, necessitating a very delicate and fiddley repair.

On the majority of cloisonné pieces, large areas are just glazed enamel, and the wire is only used in the places of decoration. This means that if you are lucky, the repair may well be just a matter of replacing the enamel, and as this is the easiest kind of cloisonné repair, we will deal with it first.

The procedure is to first remove any loose enamel that may

be about to drop out around the area of damage. Sometimes, hairline cracks radiate from the point of impact, while the enamel is still quite firm, and this poses the problem of just how far to go with removing the enamel. If you are not careful you could take off far too much, and give yourself a much bigger job than necessary.

Take care then, that you just remove the enamel that is actually loose. In most cases, this will be obvious, and there will be a clearly defined border around the damage, but when you are not sure, test with the tip of your razor knife where the enamel meets the metal. If it moves easily, remove it, if not, leave it alone.

Admittedly, the hairline cracks are very difficult to hide, but there are a few ways, which we will come to soon.

Having cleaned the wound, so to speak, there are two ways of going about the repair depending on the colour, and the thickness of the glaze. On a dull colour with a thin glaze it is possible to repair the same as for champlevé, with quick setting plastic and plastic enamel paint. This usually applies only to the older examples of cloisonné, eighteenth-century or before, and the multi-coloured type where a repair is easily hidden.

It is far more likely that the piece will have a deep, translucent glaze, more typical of the nineteenth-century type, as earlier pieces seldom come on to the market.

With this kind of deep glaze, of course, we come back to the old problem of broken glass, i.e., because it is translucent you can see the join. In some cases, this problem is impossible to surmount, and the best you can hope to do is a neat repair that may not stand up to close scrutiny, but will not stand out like a sore thumb on the mantelpiece three feet away.

To do this type of repair you will need a cold enamelling kit. There are a lot of these on the market at craft shops, but the one I use is Enamelcraft. If Enamelcraft is unavailable in your area, any similar plastic or acrylic substance will do as well.

118

Basically, this is the same type of liquid plastic used for encapsulating insects, jewellery etc., and for making paperweights. It sets very hard and is practically scratch proof. Both opaque and translucent paints are provided, so colours and glazes can be very evenly matched.

Apart from the so called 'fish-scale' type of cloisonne, which we will deal with next, a base colour will be needed to hide the copper exposed by the removal of the damaged enamel. Even the opaque pigments do not seem to hide this completely, so the first job is to match the colour with your plastic enamel paints. When doing this, be careful just to paint the copper, and not the edges of the enamel. The exposed part of the edge is about half colour and half glaze, and a clear glaze to clear glaze join looks far better than if there is paint in between.

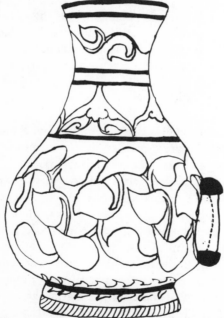

Fig. 18. A Plasticene wall is built around the damaged area to achieve the correct curve.

Having painted the copper you have two possible courses of action. If the surface to match is a medium glaze, the opaque pigments will give the best results, or if it is the deep, translucent type, you will need the translucent pigments to give the depth. Like everything else, a little practice on some expendable surface will pay dividends.

The kit provides tin-foil mixing dishes which are very handy, but take great care to mix the plastic and hardener in exactly the proportions recommended; they are fairly critical.

Most likely the repair will be on the curved side or body of the vase, bowl or plate, so the area will need overfilling to obtain the curve. The plastic therefore has to be contained, and to do this we come back to our most simple and useful aid to restoration, plasticene. Build a plasticene wall around the area about a quarter of an inch larger than the hole in the enamel, and make it high enough to achieve the right curve.

Press the plasticene down hard on to the surface of the cloisonné so that the liquid plastic cannot seep underneath before it sets.

Having made the wall and mixed the liquid plastic and pigments to your liking, prop the cloisonné piece up so that the damaged area is level and pour in the plastic.

This is another one of those overnight jobs, as the plastic takes a few hours to set. In the morning therefore, remove the plasticene wall and carefully file the plastic to shape.

When you start filing, you will notice that the surface of the plastic will whiten where the file scratches it, but do not worry about it, file it down slightly oversize with the 8 in round file, and then finish it with 320 followed by 600 wet-and-dry.

The final surface is achieved by removing the scratches made by the abrasives, and the best thing for this is metal polish and a lot of elbow power. Finally the surface of the plastic comes up like glass to match the surrounding glaze of the cloisonné.

Care must be taken during this operation not to scratch the enamel around the damage with the wet-and-dry. This is only too easy to do, and the result will be a smooth, glasslike surface where you have done the repair, surrounded by a halo of dull enamel.

In case you manage to achieve this unfortunate effect, the only answer is to literally polish it out, and this is best done with the type of polish used for painted metal surfaces, available from auto supply shops. I usually do it whilst watching television. The action of applying the polish and then rubbing

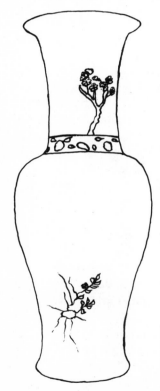

Fig. 19. Absorbing cracks into a flower pattern

it off soon becomes automatic, and at the end of one or two programs, it is done.

Having finished the repair, there may still be the hair-line cracks we spoke about earlier radiating outwards from the damage. Although it does not appear so, these cracks do have a slight gap. Not enough to fill with clear plastic, but enough for dirt to seep down. On dark surfaces they may hardly show, and are therefore probably best left alone, but on

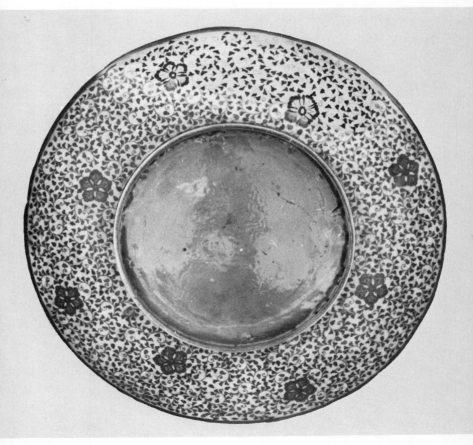

16. A repair on the reverse side of a cloisonné plate, almost complete with the key pattern finished and a few leaves still to paint in

surfaces where they are only too apparent, there are two little dodges that will sometimes solve the problem.

Number one is the same as with some pottery cracks, and that is simply to bleach the dirt out. This often makes them fade into insignificance.

In cases where they still offend the eye, take a good look at the patterned section of the piece, and see if you can visualize what another section of similar pattern would look like superimposed on the repair. In this way, the cracks can often become stems of flowers, or be absorbed into a pattern of some other nature.

If you decide to do this, the best way to go about it is to paint the coloured part of the pattern first, and then paint a simulation of the wire around them. In the case of a floral pattern, which is very common in cloisonné, paint the leaves, petals and blossoms first, in their respective colours, join them up with the branches, stems or whatever, copying carefully from the existing decoration, and then border them last of all. This is much easier than trying to paint the wire borders first with no guideline to go by.

A good example of the reproduction of a floral pattern is Photo 16. This is the reverse side of a large Chinese plate.

Oddly enough, the front of the plate was virtually undamaged in this instance, but the entire lighter area on the back was missing all the enamel and wire. Just the bare copper was left to work from.

Being Chinese cloisonné, the enamel was opaque, like champlevé. The colour was a particular shade of beige that was available in plastic-enamel paint, so in this case I replaced the missing enamel with quick setting plastic. This plate, incidentally was 15 inches in diameter, so the area to repair was quite large.

Having smoothed down the plastic to the level of the surrounding enamel, I painted on the base colour and left it to dry. You will notice that the pattern is of a few large blossoms which form the key, and hundreds of leaves linked by spiralling branches forming the background.

By careful measurement, the large blossoms were located on their correct spots, and the pattern gradually built up from there, again marking the key points out by measurement.

At the time the photo was taken, the pattern is almost complete, lacking only the smaller leaves in between the spirals, and in this case, because the plate was an old one, it needed 'spotting' in the same way as champlevé.

Naturally, as the wire is very thin, it is far from easy to reproduce a fair likeness of it. When I first tried this task I thought it was impossible, I just could not get the wire thin enough or straight enough. I eventually found that the secret lies in having the right kind of brush, and having a lot of practice. It is amazing what you can achieve if you are determined enough.

Oddly enough, a long-haired brush is better at thin, straight lines than a short one. I found this out from a coach painter who often had to paint long, straight lines freehand. The hairs on the brush he used for this purpose were about two inches in length, and the metal sleeve that held them was about 3/16 in diameter. Scaling this down for the size of the lines I wanted, I ended up with a good quality sable brush with the hair about an inch long, tapering to a point and held by a collar of about 3/32 in diameter, which is in between 1/16 and $\frac{1}{8}$ inch. This does the majority of wire simulation, but I do have another one trimmed down to just two or three hairs for the really fine wires.

Fortunately, a lot of cloisonné is multi-coloured, making your job a lot easier. the reds, browns, yellows, greens and pale blues etc., are all quite easy to match. The smaller vases with the highly intricate and delicate patterns are sometimes very difficult. Not impossible mind you, but awkward and fiddley to say the least. Practice shows you where your limitations are *at first*. Limitations, however can be overcome like most obstacles, and you will be surprised how you improve with each job, and gain increasing familiarity with the use of materials.

We mentioned earlier a type of cloisonné known as 'fish scale', which is so called because in between areas of wire decoration there are panels that closely resemble fish scale under a clear, translucent glaze. It is quite easy to simulate this by laying a piece of silver paper against the exposed copper and impressing the pattern in it. This is what the original maker did, and the method of repair is the same.

Cut out a piece of silver paper, from a cigarette packet or similar, to the exact shape of the hole. This has to be really accurate, because any discrepancies will show up with annoying clarity through the glaze.

The 'fish-scale' effect can be achieved by pressing a suitably sized blunt object on to the silver paper, and forming the resulting indentations in to the desired pattern. The size of the blunt object depends on the size of the 'fish scales', so you will have to improvise. Two things I have found useful for this job are the end of a pencil or paint brush. With the pencil, for example, providing it is a round one, if you press just one side of the end in to the silver paper, you will produce a small arc. If you link a number of arcs together to form a line, and then do another line underneath so that the centre of each arc comes under the join on the top line of arcs, (like a bricklayer builds a wall) and then a third line with the arcs corresponding to the top line and a fourth corresponding to the second and so on, this will build up a fish scale pattern. The size of the arc you want will govern the size of tool used to produce them.

The beauty of this particular repair is that you do not need to add the glaze until you are completely satisfied with the pattern, so you can have as many attempts as you like. Be careful though, to be gentle with the silver paper, it tears very easily.

It may be, that the vase you are repairing just has a lump of glaze missing, and the fish scale is still in place. If this is the case, or if you have just finished patterning the silver paper, all you now have to do is to mix up some clear glaze according to instructions, and while it is settling for a few minutes to let the bubbles out, build a plasticene wall (*see* fig. 18) as before and then pour in the plastic.

While you are leaving it to set, make sure to prop the vase so that the plastic is absolutely level and unable to move. it is also a good idea to cover it with a sheet of paper to ensure that no dust can get into it before it cures.

Like all plastics, there is a certain amount of shrinkage, so make sure you overfill the damaged area. It is quite easy to file down, and only takes a few minutes, but it you have to add more, you have to wait for it to cure before you can start again.

Before leaving this section, I would like to stress once more the importance of getting the proportions of plastic and hardener just right. A handy measuring jug is provided with the kit to help you with this, so follow the instructions meticulously.

Temperature also plays a part in the curing process, and if left in a cold room overnight it may well not set hard, or not hard enough to work with a file anyway, so always test it with the tip of your razor knife before removing the plasticene wall. If it has not hardened at all, you may have got the mixture wrong, nevertheless, it may still set if left in a warm place, the airing cupboard for instance, for a further twenty-four hours. The same applies if it is quite firm, but still a bit rubbery. The rule is, do not start to work on it until it is rock hard, even if you have to wait a few days. In fact, the longer you can leave it, the better.

In nearly all cases, the decoration in cloisonné will be on the surface, so that if you run your fingers over it you can feel it. This makes it very convenient for building up the base colour and shape, and painting the pattern on the top. Occasionally though, you may come across what I call a 'half-and-half' piece. In this type, the enamel and wire part must have been made first, and then the whole lot covered in a clear glaze.

When you repair this kind of cloisonné, there is no reason why you should not proceed in the same way. Underfill the damaged area with the base coat, paint on the decoration and then over fill it with clear glaze and finish off as before. If you do not do it this way, the repairs will not look realistic.

Careful observation of this kind of detail, and the little finishing touches you sometimes need, like dulling down the glaze to match the original texture, if necessary, can turn a good repair into a perfect one.

Cloisonné Lamps. Like pottery vases, the neck of a cloisonné vase is vulnerable to damage, and is sometimes broken beyond the possibility of repair, especially when the copper is badly dented out of shape. Whereas a dent in the body of the vase can be filled and decorated and therefore hidden, the inside of the neck is only too visible.

A very slight dent right in the lip of the vase can sometimes be panel beaten out, but usually at the price of dislodging quite a lot of the enamel, which makes the attempt rather impractical. Besides, most pieces have a copper or brass moulding forming a rim around the top to finish it off nicely, and once this is pulled out of shape or dented, it is impossible to repair nicely.

Should just this rim be damaged, of course, there is no reason why a new one should not be made up by a machine shop and used as a replacement, provided the original rim can be detached. On some vases they are part of the copper base that forms the whole vase, and on others they are soldered at the top. Only with the latter kind is it feasible to remove it without causing too much damage to the enamel in the vicinity.

Mostly, when the neck of a vase has been the point of

impact in an accident, more than just the rim will be damaged, while the rest of the vase may be in perfect condition. In this event, it is a pity to throw it away, or keep it on display with an ugly area of damage around the neck when it could very likely be made into a very attractive lamp.

Lack of size seems to be no handicap, I have frequently been called upon by customers to convert vases into lamps when they are only four or five inches in height.

With lamps of this size, the major problem is one of stability, and this can be achieved by filling the vase with sand, or better still, lead shot, and sticking it to a carved, Oriental hardwood base. These bases are now being imported in a whole range of sizes and sold at quite a lot of antique shops, especially those specializing in Oriental antiques. Better still, of course, is to acquire a proper antique rosewood stand, but this is liable to cost a lot more than a reproduction, and the particular size you want may take a bit of tracking down.

Brass light fittings, which in my opinion look better than plastic ones, are becoming more difficult to buy, but a good electrical suppliers can usually get them for you in both the normal and miniature sizes. One good tip is to ask around your friends, because these are the kind of things that people hoard in boxes with all kinds of other odds and ends in their garages and toolsheds. Sometimes, if you are successful in this way, the fittings are quite old, and made of real brass, and these look a lot better than the more modern nickel-brass type. This type of electrical fitting is not used in modern equipment, and is therefore redundant for normal domestic use.

The actual cutting off of the damaged neck has to be done with great care. Enamel never forms a very good bond with the copper, and being brittle, is inclined to chip off and crack, especially when there is no wire to support it.

First, a decision has to be made where to cut. To a certain extent this will depend on the downward extent of the damage. Naturally the cut has to be below this, but as with the pottery lamp, pattern is another deciding factor. You do not want to cut right through a pattern if half an inch below there is a nice line to go by.

Having marked your cutting line with a felt-tipped pen, bind the area immediately below with tape, as tight as you can get it, to help hold the enamel in place.

Now get out your grinding equipment, select a sharp, new, miniature wheel for the flexible drive, and cut carefully around the line down as far as the copper. Do not try to cut through the copper, or you will quickly blunt the wheel. The copper should now be visible all the way around. This is important. The cut should have completely separated the enamel on the top part that you wish to remove, from the bottom part that is to remain. If, in some places you are not quite through to the bare copper, go back and grind away the remaining enamel.

The next step calls for confidence and a hacksaw with a very sharp blade. The smaller or junior type of hacksaw is preferable as it has finer teeth.

Hold the vase very firmly pressed down on its side on to a folded blanket or piece of foam rubber and start sawing gently around the exposed copper. As soon as you break through, turn the vase around so you are always sawing from the top. Use your saw as though you are cutting through soft butter and do not want to get through too quickly.

Most of the strength in a moulded object is in its shape. The normal trumpet shaped top together with the moulded lip keep the place you are cutting nice and firm. As you cut through, however, this firmness goes, and if you press too hard, or catch the blade in the metal on a back-stroke, the copper will flex and pieces of enamel will be dislodged. Hence, keep the blade working from the outside by turning the vase as soon as it is through the copper, and you will greatly reduce the likelihood of this happening. The tape will also help to hold everything in place, and so with reasonable care you can end up with a nice clean cut, no cracks and no chips over an eighth of an inch deep. (It is practically impossible to do this job without chipping the edge of the enamel slightly.)

When you have cut off the neck there are two or three alternative methods of completing the job, depending on how much time you have and how much you want to spend.

The quickest and easiest method is to cut out a cardboard disc that fits tightly into the neck of the vase, push it down about a quarter of an inch, and fill the top up with quick setting plastic. This can then be levelled off, a hole drilled in the centre to take the pillar of the light fitting, which is then stuck in with a little more plastic on the thread. The plastic painted gold or some suitable colour, and that is it! Any chips in the enamel around the top can be filled at the same time, and the gold paint extended down about a quarter of an inch.

The pillar I mentioned for the light fitting (*see* fig. 20) is a short brass tube of about half an inch, with two different diameters meeting half way along, each with its own thread. The larger end screws up into the light fitting, and the smaller end fits into the lamp. The fact that this end is threaded is irrelevant as far as we are concerned, as it is just as easily stuck into position. If, for some reason of your own you would prefer to be able to unscrew it when you want, this is quite easy with the first method. Just grease the thread with vaseline before setting it into the quick setting plastic, and when the plastic has hardened, you will have made your own screw thread.

In most cases, the lamp shade you use will cover the light fitting area up, so its appearance, whilst needing to be neat, is not critical. In some lamps, however, especially if they are for re-sale, something a little more professional is required.

The cap that I have illustrated, (fig. 20) is the type I normally use. It is turned out of quarter-inch brass on a lathe. One of the chief advantages of a cap like this is that it fits

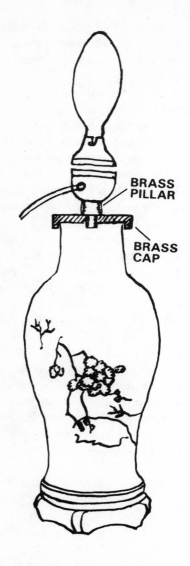

BRASS
PILLAR

BRASS
CAP

Fig. 20. A brass cap suitable for lamp making

down an eighth of an inch or so over the edge of the enamel, and so it covers any slight chipping that might have occurred during cutting.

A local machine shop makes up these caps for me for about seventy-five cents apiece, including the brass. I supply the outside diameter of the neck, and for the first few I gave them a diagram as well to show them what I wanted. They also drill the hole for the post, so all that is left for me to do is to ballast the vase with lead shot or sand, stick the brass cap on, stick the threaded post into the hole, and screw the light fitting on.

I do not normally like putting work out, because once in the hands of other people, delays inevitably occur. after all, you

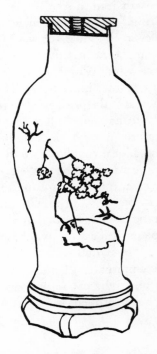

Fig. 21. A plug made from quick-setting plastic

can hardly expect a busy machine shop to drop everything for a seventy-five-cent job. It does, however, finish the job off very well, and is, I think, well worth the wait and the expense.

For those with woodworkers lathes, there is absolutely no reason why you should not turn up a similar cap in wood. Black plastic enamel paint can simulate an ebonised surface and make it look very authentic.

Another method is to make up a plasticene mould, and make a top in the form of a plug out of quick-setting plastic. (*see* fig. 21). In this way, you can make a lip around the top, which gives the whole thing a better appearance.

Even half filled with lead, a small vase does not make an extremely stable lamp. Although I am normally very much against drilling holes in things, if the vase is to be stuck to a carved base there can be no disadvantage in drilling a hole through both for the wire. Wire trailing down the side is all very well for a larger vase, but may easily lead to pulling a small one over, whereas if the wire goes up through the centre this is far less likely to happen. Make sure that the wire is a very tight fit through the base, or the sand is liable to leak out, and remember to thread it through before sticking the top on!

The switch, on large vases can be of the type included in the light fitting. In this case, fumbling around for it in the dark is not likely to upset it, but with any small lamp, it is far better to use a torpedo type switch further down the wire, away from the lamp, or better still a wall switch, so you do not have to go anywhere near it to switch on.

Like its pottery counterpart, a lamp is preferable, in value, to a restored vase, and whereas it will not ever regain the value it had before being broken, it may not be so very much less.

11
Conclusion

Restoring is the kind of business you can never learn fully, because there are always repairs that you have not come across before, new materials coming on to the market, and new techniques to try out, which is what makes it so interesting.

From a business angle there is plenty of work available due to a chronic shortage of restorers, and the breakages that are taking place all the time. It is getting harder and harder for the collector and dealer alike to buy pieces in perfect condition, so naturally the good pieces are going up rapidly in price. Both these factors are making a well restored piece a more attractive proposition than it used to be.

The price you charge is a personal matter really, and depends largely on the quality of your work. You can either charge a fair price by the hour, or give a quote. In the latter case, which is usually more acceptable to a customer, especially a new customer, always quote about twice the price you first think of. From bitter personal experience I can tell you that the job nearly always takes twice as long as you thought it would, and in this way you can still come out with a profit.

Quoting is always rather a gamble until you get to know how long the various jobs take, and the materials involved. You will probably find with your regular customers that after a while they will just give you the work to do, and accept the charge, as long as you are fair with them. The thing to bear in mind, is that the customer seldom has any idea of the time involved in some of the more fiddley jobs, so if you get a piece in to repair that you know will cost considerably more than usual, let your customer know before you start. It may well be that the piece does not have the value to justify the expense, and it is embarrassing all round to find this out afterwards!

The business can be approached in two ways, either to do repairs for other people, and charge accordingly, or to buy broken items cheaply, with a view to repairing and then selling them.

Personally, I prefer to work by the former method, which I consider to be a far safer way of making a living, but if you decide to do both, or adopt the second course, I would advise you to first get to know what the various repairs are going to cost. Secondly, get to know the type of pieces that due to their shape or texture repair really well. Thirdly, get to know your values, so you at least buy at the right price, and lastly bear in mind that a restored item will not regain its original value.

I have always looked upon restoring as a sort of cottage industry, and a good way of stepping out of the 'rat race'. It can also be a pleasant hobby, or a profitable one, or both. It is the sort of work that calls for fairly constant improvisation. Admittedly, some of the jobs are a bit tedious, but I doubt very much if any occupation is not, at some time or other.

The reason a lot of people will not attempt a repair is because they make up their minds they are incapable of doing it, and yet most of these jobs are a lot easier than you might think, and require patience rather than skill. The skill comes later, with practice. Few people start off anything as experts, we all have to start somewhere. I believe the first hurdle is to adopt the mental attitude that you can do it, and not only that, but you will. Do not worry about initial mistakes, they have all been made before by other people, just cultivate the determination to succeed, and you will.

There are few limits to the uses these materials can be put to, they are very versatile. I have done successful repairs to papier-maché, Oriental lacquer work, Tunbridge Ware boxes, clock cases, ornate mirror surrounds, cast iron urns and furniture where a knob or something similar has been kocked off. By the methods described, the colours and textures of a wide range of materials can be simulated, and where necessary moulds can be used to reproduce complex shapes. The more you get used to using and handling these materials, the more ideas will probably occur to you about other possible uses.

In this book, I have tried to give at least one example of each type of repair you are likely to come across. It is not always necessary to use the repair material I have described, however. For instance, there is absolutely no reason why the make-or-break kit materials should not be used for filling up chips in plates or cups etc. In fact, if you are repairing pottery you actually use for eating, it would be preferable to use this kit so that the piece may be fired in the oven. In this way the resulting glaze will be hard enough to withstand the onslaught of abrasion by knives and forks, and the washing up water. One of the other purposes of this kit is to enable you to buy plain, undecorated crockery, which is usually cheaper, and do your own personal decorating, from an initial or symbol to as complex a pattern as you choose. This is then glazed and baked firmly in place.

With the more complex moulding, like heads etc., there are other kinds of liquid plastic equally suitable. With the Enamelcraft kit, for instance, it is sometimes possible to include the base colour and therefore save having to apply this afterwards.

No doubt you will develop your own techniques and preferences for certain materials as you go along, and I hope the materials and ideas in this book provide a useful starting point for you.

Appendix:
List of Manufacturers
and Mail-Order Suppliers

The products and materials mentioned in this book should be available, for the most part, from local hardware stores and arts-and-crafts stores. However, if these shops cannot fill your needs, the mail-order suppliers listed here can. In many cases the listed outlets carry stock beyond that which we have mentioned; we have only included products pertaining to our text. In very specialized situations, you may contact a manufacturer directly for distribution information.

Adhesive Products Corporation
1660 Boone Avenue
Bronx, New York 10460
    Manufacturers of Adrub RTV rubber mold compound

Boin Arts and Crafts
87 Morris Street
Morristown, New Jersey 07960
    Artist's supplies, ceramic putty and plastic, enamel glazes, hand tools, non-firing enamels, plastic foam

Arthur Brown & Brother, Inc.
2 West 46th Street
New York, New York 10036
    Adhesives, airbrushes, artist's supplies, ceramic putty, gold leaf, enamel glazes, quick-setting plastic, artist's knives, rubber mold materials

Castolite
P. O. Box 391
Woodstock, Illinois 60098
    Casting compounds, plastic fillers

138

Delco Craft Center, Inc.
30081 Stephenson Highway
Madison Heights, Missouri
48071
Artist's supplies, ceramic supplies, cold enamels, glazes, kiln accessories, plastic compounds

Devcon Corporation
Danvers, Massachusetts 01923
Manufacturers of various epoxies and adhesives

Floquil, Inc.
Cobleskill, New York 12043
Manufacturers of various paints and cold enamels

Magic Marker Corporation
Glendale, New York 11227
Manufacturers of air brushes

Minnesota Clay
8001 Grand Avenue South
Bloomington, Minnesota 55420
Glazes

Ohio Ceramic Supply, Inc.
P. O. Box 630
2861 State Route 59
Kent, Ohio 44240
Ceramic supplies, glazes, tools

Sculpture Services, Inc.
9 East 19th Street
New York, New York 10003
Casting plastics, potter's plasters, mold rubber

Thomas C. Thompson
1539 Old Deerfield Road
Highland Park, Illinois 60035
Enamel colors

Zim's
P. O. Box 7620
Salt Lake City, Utah 84107
Enamel paints, gold leaf, resin craft supplies

Index